MIRACLE
ON MARKET

Where Hope Is Found and Change Happens

Jay P. Davidson

IGNITE
P R E S S
Fresno, CA

Published in the United States by
Ignite Press
5070 N. Sixth St. #189
Fresno, CA 93710
www.IgnitePress.us

ISBN: 978-1-953655-78-3 (Amazon Print)
ISBN: 978-1-953655-79-0 (IngramSpark) PAPERBACK
ISBN: 978-1-953655-80-6 (Ebook)

For bulk purchase and for booking, contact:

Jay P. Davison, MSSW, ACSW, LCSW, LCADC, MAC
Jay.Davidson@TheHealingPlace.org
1020 W. Market Street, Louisville, KY 40202

Library of Congress Control Number: 2021906465

Cover design by Kathleen Cantwell
Edited by Emma Hatcher
Interior design by Jetlaunch Layout Services

THE HEALING PLACE

This book is dedicated to those affected and afflicted by addiction.

Acknowledgments

I thank my wonderful wife, Jackie, for her love and continuing support of my commitment to The Healing Place and for always encouraging me and challenging me to follow God's will for me and for us.

A special thanks to Dan Caudill, Jesse Bollinger, and Phil Marshall for providing the financial support for my story.

A special thanks to Billy Reed for his technical editing expertise and his unique insight and support helping me become open and vulnerable to share the emotional side of my story.

I give special recognition to Dr. Will W. Ward Jr. and Dr. Kenneth Peters for their vision to address drug and alcohol addiction within the homeless community. Without their untiring support, The Healing Place would not be what it is today.

I thank Chris Fajardo for his counsel, mentoring, and experience, strength, and hope as we built the foundation of the abstinence-based, long-term residential, peer-driven social model recovery program.

I thank Cathy Fyock, The Business Book Strategist, for guiding me through the challenge of writing this book. She encouraged me to keep writing.

With sincere gratitude I thank my volunteer editors: Dr. Will W. Ward Jr., Dan Caudill, Kayla Pierce, Lelan Woodmansee, and

Jan Karzan. I thank Marla Highbaugh and Laci Comer for their many hours of editing and formatting the manuscript.

Finally, I acknowledge that, throughout my entire life, my Higher Power, whom I call Christ Jesus, was and is guiding me through life. I recognize that every difficult challenge as well as every success was preparing me to reach out and help another suffering alcoholic and addict.

CONTENTS

PREFACE

I often ask myself, "How in the world did I get here?"

For the last three decades, I have had the pleasure of watching men and women challenge the demon known as addiction and begin a new life in recovery. Their story of sobriety wouldn't be possible without my own—and what a story that is.

My journey is one that winds through Vietnam, Germany, Saudi Arabia, Israel, and military bases around the United States and the world . . . and even a carnival. It's a journey filled with the highest of highs and the lowest of lows. From feeling on top of the world to the pit of despair, my story is an implausible one, I admit, but my story is one that is crafted by God's love and His will for me.

I wouldn't have it any other way.

PROLOGUE

I have often shared my experience, strength, and hope at twelve-step meetings over my thirty-six years of sobriety. Many know some parts of my history, but few know the whole story. This book is the first time that I have put together a complete picture of who Jay Davidson truly is.

In recent years, I have been asked on occasion to write down my story. When sharing my story, I start by saying that every experience, whether good or bad, has given me the faith, trust, and courage to help another alcoholic or addict who is on their journey to recovery.

I have to say that my twenty-eight years at The Healing Place has been a spiritual journey guided by all the men and women who have walked through the doors of The Healing Place, seeking a spiritual awakening or experience. I am forever grateful for all the lessons I have learned from these remarkable individuals.

I am grateful to be blessed with the most fantastic staff ever assembled to build and sustain the social model recovery program. Thanks in large part to the leadership, guidance, and support provided by all of the board members over the years, the social model recovery program has flourished. We have achieved unbelievable goals of growth and success! This success of The Healing Place is directly related to the passion, commitment, and spirituality of the alumni, clients, staff, and members of the board. I am grateful for each one.

I'm writing this book to share my experiences and thoughts about the traditional residential, long-term, social model recovery program in hopes that this model, in its current form, will be sustained and maintained long after I am gone. When there is a need to help another suffering alcoholic and or addict, the traditional model of The Healing Place will be there to answer that desperate cry for help.

CHAPTER 1

PRESENT DAY

It is 8:25 a.m. on a Friday. I walk out of the Davidson Administration Building of The Healing Place. Did I say, Davidson Administrative Building? That's right. Not in my wildest dreams did I ever think that I would have a building named after me. It was a complete surprise. I believe that it's the only secret that The Healing Place board members, staff, clients, or my wife ever kept from me. The day of the dedication was an emotional event filled with love from everyone present. The dedication filled my heart with love and gratitude for the privilege of being part of this miracle called The Healing Place. I could not stop crying.

Now, standing in front of the Davidson Administration Building, I am watching eighty men with backpacks start trudging to Fourth and St. Catherine to the Healing Center. It is an impressive sight to see; men committed to walking on the path of recovery. I can not help but be proud of their determination and dedication to seek sobriety. As I continue to watch these men trudge, they pass what used to be an auto parts store and is now the Brady Center, a facility operated by The Healing Place that provides transitional housing and support services to men being released from prison. Knowing the hardship and challenges of prison life, I am grateful that these men have an opportunity for a new start in life.

Now it is 9 a.m., and I see men and women entering the original detox building, 1017 and 1019 West Market, to attend the morning three-hour intensive outpatient group. Recovery Louisville is an expansion of services to reach out to the alcoholic and addict that is seeking sobriety but has social support systems in place to allow them to continue working while accessing recovery services on an outpatient basis. This outpatient service is a complimentary service to the long-term, residential, peer-driven social model of recovery.

It is now 10:15 a.m., and the men in the long-term recovery program are taking a break in the courtyard of the new building at 1020 West West Market. The men had just attended a community meeting and are taking a break before their next class. I pinch myself and shake my head, thinking I am dreaming. Directly in front of me is a 102,000 square foot building with four stories, providing services for 425 men. It is a beautiful blessing to see men having the opportunity to achieve sobriety and have a meaningful and productive life. I honestly cannot comprehend the magnitude and significance of this accomplishment for The Healing Place. This is unquestionably God at work, giving men a chance for a new life—one without alcohol or drugs.

On this Friday, I am excited about tomorrow's celebration of recovery at the annual alumni reunion that will happen at the women's campus at Fifteenth and Hill. The women's campus is another miracle from God, where 250 women are finding their way to sobriety and a meaningful and productive life. For me, the reunion is a celebration of family where alumni bring their children and come to celebrate recovery with each other. It is my family. I love and rejoice in their sobriety and success. I have the joy of presenting plaques to the male and female Alumni of the Year as voted by all the clients and alumni. I also recognize The Healing Place Volunteer of the Year. I am blessed to give and receive all the love that is shared this day. A special part of the reunion is that I present bronze Healing Place tokens to those alumni who have achieved eighteen months of sobriety. It is a lot of fun, and it warms my heart to see all the smiling, loving faces full of life.

I feel like I am in a dream state of life. How in the world did I get here? Well, it is a story that winds its way through Vietnam, Germany, Saudi Arabia, Israel, and several military bases around the world. It is an implausible story, I admit, but one where every step was crafted by God's love and His will for me.

It began in Colorado . . .

CHAPTER 2

MY DARKEST HOUR

It was a routine Monday morning. I was heading into the office at Fort Knox, Kentucky, to continue planning for the upcoming summer camp program for 6,000 ROTC cadets who were coming to complete eight weeks of training. This training would allow them to enter the ROTC program at their university as a junior. I had just returned from Fort Bragg, North Carolina, where my commanding officer and I had briefed the general staff about the camp their college students would be attending. I felt that the briefing went great and my boss was pleased. I walked into my office as usual at 6 a.m., but I knew right away that this was going to be a different day. My immediate supervisor was sitting at my desk, waiting for me. He never was in the office before 10 a.m., so I immediately began to sweat and got very nervous. Something was drastically wrong, but I didn't know what it was—I was in a panic and full of fear.

My supervisor removed all doubt when he said, "The general says that, if you don't get a handle on your alcoholism, he will kick you out of the Army in forty-five days!"

My world seemed to be crashing down around me. I broke out in a cold sweat and almost passed out. How did the general find out that I was an alcoholic? I continued to panic. I didn't know what to do. I thought back to the previous weekend: I vaguely remembered that the general and I flew back together on Sunday morning from Fayetteville, North Carolina. We had traveled in our Class A uniform and been seated side by side. I think that I remember having a couple of drinks or so but didn't notice that I had spilled a drink on my uniform. All I knew that morning was that the general was taking my lifelong dream away from me. How could he be so cruel?

I had been in JROTC in high school and was very successful at it, becoming the cadet battalion commander. My dream was to retire as a lieutenant colonel in the United States Army. At that very moment, I was a promotable major on the list to become a lieutenant colonel. The general was going to take that away from me. I would lose my retirement and be drummed out of the Army in disgrace! My drinking had already broken my first marriage, and I had lost custody of my two boys. Those life-changing events did not stop me from drinking, but the threat of losing my dream filled me with fear, panic, despair, and hopelessness. My life would be over; my future, black.

I felt that there was no hope. I was helpless. I went home and told my wife, who said that I needed to get into treatment immediately. My ego was so big that I replied, "I can't call for help; you must call for me." I told her to call some places to get me into treatment, but after several calls, my wife realized that I had to be the one to make those calls. I humbled myself and made the call to the only place that could help me. I entered the intensive outpatient program at the Army Community Counseling Center at Fort Knox on February 10, 1983.

CHAPTER 3

ALCOHOL BECOMES MY MISTRESS

As I reflected on my darkest hour, I realized that it all began back in my early childhood. My mom and dad had demonstrated a terrible relationship. In 1949, when I was seven years old and my sister was only four, I watched as my dad pushed my mother through a first-floor glass window while he was trying to cut the bottom off all her dresses. Dad was drunk again. And I was terrified. I attempted to stop him, but I ended up on the floor.

The next trauma that I experienced was when my dad was driving me and my sister home from the grocery store. The front right tire went flat and, in his drunken stupor, my dad continued to drive home on the rim, casting a two-foot-long stream of sparks all the way. My sister and I were terrified. I thought that the car would catch on fire. My dad left sometime later, never to be seen or heard from again. I felt abandoned and lost. I thought that it was my fault that Dad left us.

I became the man of the house and took charge of my sister, since my mom had to go to work immediately. We lived within walking distance to the elementary school, so I made sure that we made it to school on time. My mother loved us and did her very best to care for us. I took charge and excelled in being the man of the house and watching over my sister, although she didn't like that much supervision. As time went on, the three of us settled into a routine, relying only on ourselves. I felt responsible for helping take care of the family. I believed that I had a purpose and focus.

My mom thought that it was important for me to have a male role model, so we joined the local Methodist Church so that I could join the Cub Scouts. After getting into the scouts, I stopped going to church. Cub Scouts, and later Boy Scouts, saved my life. The pressure of taking care of the family started to wear on me, so the weekend scouting activities gave me a break from my family responsibilities. Once a month throughout the year, the Boy Scout troop would spend the weekend camping in the high country of Colorado. The freedom of being in the mountains and being free from the stress of family was exhilarating. I thrived in the scouts, earning skill badges to become a Life Scout. At one summer camp, I survived a three-day ordeal to become a member of the Order of the Arrow, which was a significant accomplishment. I looked up to my scout master and he became my role model. He was a wonderful father figure who I desperately needed. He taught me courage, moral values, and right from wrong. The weekend camping trips in the high country of Colorado gave me self-confidence and taught me survival skills. However, apart from my scouting experience, a darker side of my life began. At the age of thirteen, I started smoking and drinking. One of the consequences of that new behavior was that I lost interest in scouting and quit before I was about to earn the highest level of scouting, Eagle Scout.

My mother caught me smoking with some of the neighborhood boys behind the house. She wanted to teach me a lesson.

She sat me down at the kitchen table with a full pack of cigarettes and told me that I had to sit there until I had smoked every last one. While smoking the first cigarette, I thought that there was no way I was going to finish them all, so I started faking coughing and having the dry heaves in hopes that my mom would say that I had learned my lesson and didn't have to smoke any more.

Little did she know that my faking was my way of saying that I was going to smoke no matter what she did to me or told me to do. I found stress relief from smoking; it was an answer to prayer, or so I thought. I began to hang around with other boys around the neighborhood and at school who smoked. It became a ritual that gave me a feeling of belonging and a sense of camaraderie. I was introduced to beer not long after I started smoking. Back then, any beer that had an alcohol content of 3.2 percent or less was legal for eighteen-year-olds to consume. One of the neighborhood boys was able to get a six-pack of that beer and invited me to his hideout for a drink. I took my first sip and fell in love. I loved it so much that I drank two more cans. Later in life, I learned that I had a predisposition to becoming addicted to alcohol, because both my mother and father were both practicing alcoholics. I found a total escape from reality, if only for a short time. The beer was better than cigarettes, because alcohol gave me relief from the stress of family life. I had crossed over, no longer drinking for pleasure but drinking to escape from life. Drinking kept me from dealing with stress, even if just for a moment. I didn't stop smoking. Now I had two forms of relief—beer and smoking.

Even though I had found my way of dealing with life, I knew that I still had family responsibilities. I worked hard in school and made good grades, mostly A's. I enjoyed school, but my smoking and drinking sometimes got in the way. Not being very athletic, I was too slow to try out for track, not big enough for football, and I couldn't shoot a basketball, so I volunteered for Junior ROTC (JROTC). I had found where I belonged. I liked the structure and discipline that JROTC offered, and I excelled.

It was hard work, but I loved all of the training, the Drill and Ceremony, and going to the rifle range. I enjoyed learning about leadership and being in charge. My ego was exploding. I became the cadet battalion commander in the grade of lieutenant colonel during my senior year of high school. My first real date in high school was in my senior year. I asked a female cadet to be my date at the JROTC Military Ball. At the time, I thought that she said yes only because I was the cadet battalion commander. I had always had a feeling of low self-esteem, even though I was successful.

My first real job was to work as a busboy at an amusement park that had a floral garden, a summer stock off-Broadway theater, an open-air ballroom, and a bar and grill. The manager gave me the responsibility to come in at 7 a.m. every morning to receive supplies and food, then come back in the evening to bus the tables and sweep the floors. As part of my morning routine, I would go over to the ballroom and make sure that the bar was closed and that all the "last call" drink glasses were stacked up against the window. I was able to take home a lot of bar glasses for my future use. I also took the opportunity to sample any leftover drinks. I was living my dream—I was making money from my job, I had access to free alcohol, and I was smoking. Does life get any better than this?

Baby Jay with his dad.

*Last family picture
before the divorce.*

CHAPTER 4
MARRIED TOO YOUNG

I was so successful in school that in my senior year, I was only taking classes in the morning. Throughout this time, I continued to smoke and drink heavily—especially on the weekends—but still needed to support my family. During my senior year, I got a job at a local car finance company as a mail clerk and stock boy. I worked every day from noon until 5 p.m., picking up and sorting mail and filling supply requests from staff. After I graduated high school, I went to work at the car finance company full time. I enjoyed my job. I got to work with all the staff, from the president down. I thrived and worked hard to be the best stock clerk that they had ever had. I felt proud of my work ethic. I got into a groove, and it wasn't long before I received a promotion to cashier/teller, where I was responsible for processing payments from customers.

Although I was enjoying my job at the car finance company, I still had a burning desire to be in the military, so I submitted my application for an appointment to West Point Military Academy.

Now all I could do was wait. I felt that the military would be my way of showing my mom that I could be successful.

I didn't date much while in high school because I was hanging with the guys on the weekends drinking and smoking. I felt extremely awkward and clumsy around the girls at school, and I was much more comfortable around the guys. One of the guys at work decided that I needed to go on a blind date. He had a friend named Susan who he thought would be a perfect match for me. I wasn't sure that any woman would want to be with me, but my friend assured me that it would not be a problem. I was scared and apprehensive because I hadn't dated much, and I just knew that it would not work out. I was surprised when the blind date with Susan turned into a relationship. I had never experienced anything like that before. I was mesmerized and in a lovesick trance. What I learned later in life is that adult children of alcoholics recognize each other. What I thought was a lovesick trance was me finding another person who had learned how to live in the chaos of dealing with an alcoholic. Susan, my newfound love, was an adult child of alcoholics. We were a perfectly unhealthy match. While balancing my job at the car finance company and building this new relationship, I continued to drink heavily.

The most embarrassing moment of my young business career was when I received an invitation to attend the quarterly banquet meeting for all the dealerships sales representatives working in the tristate area. Before the opening cocktail hour, my co-worker challenged me to see who could drink the most before the banquet. I accepted his challenge and was not going to lose. I knew that I would win because heavy drinking was regular for me, and he didn't drink that much. I must have drunk at least four or five glasses of scotch and water before the banquet and was declared the "winner."

Unfortunately for me, the drinks did not sit well on my stomach. More than sixty people were there, including the president of my branch. Just as everyone had taken their seats at tables preset with salads and bread, I started to throw up. I tried to cover my mouth; that was not a good idea. The contents of my stomach flowed through my coat sleeves and onto the table. The sales representatives sitting next to me picked me up, took me to the bathroom, and helped me get cleaned up. While we were gone, the restaurant staff removed our table and brought in a new one, complete with fresh salads and bread. I returned to the table and the banquet resumed as if nothing had happened. I was horrified and completely embarrassed; all I wanted to do is go and hide in hopes that everyone would forget this ever happened. I prepared myself to be called into the president's office for a reprimand the next day, but nothing happened, nor did anyone say anything about the incident. I thought, "Wow, that is cool; I could get drunk like that without anyone getting upset. That must mean my drinking is okay." I was in total denial about how outrageous my behavior had been. Denial is the typical rationalization by an alcoholic.

I took this experience as a subtle confirmation that my drinking habit was acceptable. Doesn't everyone who drinks have at least one bad experience drinking? It did not affect my job performance or how my supervisor felt about my work, because, shortly after the incident at the banquet, I received another promotion. All of this reinforced my belief that I was leading a good life by having a great job, dating a good woman, and expanding my drinking experience. The promotions continued to come, and I progressed up the ladder of success at the car finance company.

My job was going well and my relationship with Susan continued to blossom, but I had not forgotten about my application for West Point. When it came time for the final interview, I had to decide whether I was going to continue with the process or drop out to get married. Because of my low self-esteem and fear of success, I knew I would not be selected to attend the prestigious military academy. I chose the relationship with the first girl I ever really dated over West Point. As it turned out, that decision was never really mine to make. I did not get selected for West Point, reaffirming my belief of being less than.

I never told anyone how much not getting the appointment to West Point hurt. I was devastated about not being selected, and I went into a state of depression. I didn't like the way I was feeling, so I turned to the one thing I could depend on—beer. I soon proposed to Susan, the only girl that had ever shown me any affection, and we were married on November 22, 1963. In hindsight, the wedding was a disaster. That morning, I was in the church basement, drinking "white lightning" with my mother and stepfather. I was in an emotional and mental fog. Just before the ceremony was about to start, we heard that President John F. Kennedy had been assassinated. I insisted that the wedding ceremony continue, but I should have seen this as an omen of our star-crossed relationship.

Shortly after I got married, my supervisor asked if I would be willing to accept a managerial position at the finance company branch in Cheyenne, Wyoming. I immediately said yes, without consulting my wife. Once again, I acted on my self-centeredness and selfishness, thinking only of my career and satisfying my ego. I didn't consider all the challenges to our new marriage. In our first year of marriage, we moved away from family, I got a new job, and my new wife had to find a job in a new town. We moved from Denver to Cheyenne to set up our new home. Naturally, I relied on my old faithful—alcohol—to help me through the chaos. We packed up everything we had and bought a small house in Cheyenne. Everything changed, except for my drinking.

CHAPTER 5

GERMANY, HERE WE COME

The time in Cheyenne, Wyoming, was exciting. It was the first time that I had lived outside Denver, I had a new wife, and I had a new home. Susan and I both liked dogs, so we decided to add Beckett, a golden fawn Great Dane puppy to our family. Work was going very well, and I had a good relationship with my supervisor. I continued to gain valuable accounting experience. Married life was good, and Susan and I continued to learn about each other and grow closer together. The only problem was that, during our marriage, my drinking kept me physically present but emotionally absent.

During the next couple of years, I began receiving letters of interest from the Selective Service that asked about my health and verified my current address. My wife and I talked about the possibility that the Army would draft me. We felt that it might happen soon, so Susan and I came up with a plan. Her father was a chief master sergeant in the Air Force, stationed in Wiesbaden,

Germany. We talked with my in-laws and decided that I would enlist in the Army for three years and be stationed in Germany for at least eighteen months before going to Vietnam. So, I enlisted in the Army's delayed entry program to report for duty after Christmas 1965. I knew that I was going to basic training starting in January 1966, and I was happy to learn that my basic training would be at Fort Bliss, Texas. Things were going great. We were able to sell the house back to the mortgage company with no penalty under the Soldiers and Sailors Relief Act. The finance company gave me a written guarantee of re-employment once my three-year term of service was over. I didn't think that life could get any better, and everything was working out for the best.

After I enlisted, Susan told me she was pregnant. I was happy but conflicted. What were we to do? Under draft regulations, I was eligible to void my enlistment and be honorably separated because I had a wife and one dependent. We discussed the pros and cons, but my ego won out. I decided to honor my enlistment and prepared to ship out to Fort Bliss on December 27, 1965. I helped Susan pack up our personal belongings, and she and the dog went to live with her grandparents in Oklahoma. We had only been married for two years, and we already had to deal with a long separation. I didn't fully appreciate what a strain this separation would place on our marriage. I was excited about joining the Army, but my wife was going to be alone dealing with life.

CHAPTER 6

PRIVATE TO SECOND LIEUTENANT

When I got to Fort Bliss, I felt like I was home. Meeting the other men in the platoon was a new experience for me, but the military structure and lifestyle came easy. I excelled in the training and demonstrated some leadership. My time in JROTC gave me an edge. The drill sergeants recognized my experience and made me a squad leader. It wasn't long before I became a platoon sergeant. I was getting recognition as a leader, and boy, was my ego soaring. It felt great. Back in Oklahoma, Susan was dealing with her pregnancy and all the emotional challenges of being alone.

About halfway through basic training, the senior drill sergeant called me into his office. I was afraid that I had screwed up. After reporting, the drill sergeant had me take a seat. He proceeded to tell me that because of my high scores on the ASVAB test and the two years of college credit from the University of Denver, I was eligible to apply for Officer Candidate School

(OCS). Having my leadership skills acknowledged made me feel appreciated. I thought, "This is it; this is my calling—an officer in the United States Army." I was on cloud nine.

I filled out the paperwork and waited for the official notification that I got into OCS before telling Susan. I knew that she would be upset but would also eventually support my decision. Communicating long distance was difficult, and I knew that I had screwed up by not discussing this life-changing decision. In my selfishness, I was doing what I wanted to do regardless of how it hurt my wife. I knew that I had put her in a place where she had to support my decision whether she liked it or not. It was not long until I received official orders accepting me into the OCS with a report class date to be determined later. The Army canceled my original eighteen-month enlistment for Germany. Instead of going to Fort Gordon, Georgia, for advanced training, I would be going to Fort Ord, California, for eight weeks. I could sense the barriers going up between Susan and me. I didn't put any effort into trying to understand her needs. Her pregnancy was going well, or at least I thought, but that was an assumption on my part since we weren't talking much. She remained in Oklahoma. I completed Basic Training and shipped out to report to Fort Ord in the middle of March 1966.

I excelled in the infantry training, and again, I felt like I had found my home. After I completed advanced training in California, I had to figure out how to get my wife to Columbus, Georgia, so she could join me there for my six months of training. Getting her to Georgia was difficult for her, because I didn't help her deal with all of the changes emotionally. She was alone with no emotional support, and I wasn't there to help. My attempt to fix things was to work out the details to make her trip less challenging.

As luck would have it, I found out that my former high school Professor of Military Science and Training (PMST) was stationed at Fort Benning. I contacted him and asked if he would be willing to provide a place for my wife to stay until I got to

Fort Benning sometime in July. He graciously agreed. In May of 1966, in her eighth month of pregnancy, Susan drove from Oklahoma to Georgia to live with my former PMST. I was utterly ignorant about what I was asking my wife to do: find a home for our dog, then travel 800 miles to start a new life and give birth in a strange town with no family support. All I was thinking about was me wanting my family with me while training to become an officer.

I was still in hold-over status at Fort Ord because my OCS class date had yet to be assigned. In mid-June, my wife went into premature labor and went to the local hospital in Georgia. The Red Cross immediately notified me through priority channels, and I was able to fly home. When I got there, my wife and child were both in crisis. I got to the hospital shortly after Erik was born. He was born with a severe lung disorder and was on oxygen and in an incubator. All I could do was stand there and watch him struggle to breathe. I felt helpless and hopeless. My heart was breaking. I was overcome with guilt, knowing that if my wife were still in Oklahoma, she would not have gone into premature labor and my son would not be fighting for his life.

Understandably, Susan was hysterical one moment and in total depression the next. Erik was in an incubator, struggling to breathe while under ultraviolet light because he was jaundiced. I could not hold him; all I could do was stand there and cry. Erik's lungs were failing. Sadly, Erik died thirty-six hours after he was born. I felt that God had abandoned us and that there was a part of my life that would never heal. Susan went into postpartum depression and remained in the hospital for three weeks. I was devastated and in shock. A mental fog took over, causing me to feel nothing. I was alone when I buried Erik in a donated family plot in Columbus, Georgia.

The very next day, I reported to Fort Benning to begin my training in Company 66 of the OCS Training Brigade. I was restricted to the barracks for eleven weeks. After a three-week stay in the hospital, my wife returned to live with my former

PMST until I graduated from OCS. The training was tough. The challenges were twenty-four hours a day, seven days a week. Later in the training cycle, we were allowed time on weekends to meet with our wives to go shopping, do laundry, or go out to dinner. There was little time spent with family. I never took the opportunity to have a meaningful and serious talk with my wife to give her a chance to express her pain. I couldn't face it myself, and I knew that I couldn't deal with her suffering. More barriers went up.

Out of the original company of 200 candidates, only one hundred graduated. I was commissioned to second lieutenant on December 15, 1966, and received orders to report back to Fort Ord to be a Basic Training unit officer. Susan and I packed up what belongings we had accumulated and moved back to California. I was motivated and excited to start my Army career. While I focused on moving to California, Susan felt the burden of moving and setting up a new home. Physically she was okay, but mentally she was struggling more than I knew.

The move to California was our first real experience as a married couple in the military. It was both exciting and scary. We were lucky to get housing on post as a second lieutenant. After going through in-processing and getting the house organized, I reported to my new Basic Training Company. I was not sure what I would be doing but knew that I would be busy. I quickly learned that both my company commander and the executive officer were aviators and had no real desire to run the Company. Since I had just recently graduated from OCS, I was well trained and knowledgeable of FM 22-5 Drill and Ceremony. I was the most logical person to take the 200 trainees in the company to training every day. I ran the company while the company commander and the executive officer played golf. My training day often lasted twelve hours or more, but I was in my element. The power of command was intoxicating. I was thriving and growing in confidence and self-esteem. For the first time, I was somebody.

Life is never easy. Shortly after getting settled into a routine, doctors diagnosed my wife with mononucleosis. She was sick for three months, and, between my work hours and her illness, our marriage suffered. To deal with the stress of command and Susan's health, I began drinking more and more. My wife was bedridden for those three months. I couldn't deal with everything, so I self-medicated with alcohol. Our relationship slowly deteriorated. I had a good learning experience running the company but was at a loss as to how to make my marriage better. We were at Fort Ord without family or any other support system, and I was too proud to reach out and ask for help. I thought that time would heal our loss.

After working as the Basic Training unit officer for six months, I received orders to ship out to South Vietnam. I had a thirty-day leave to relocate my wife back to Oklahoma and to report to Oakland Army Depot before I was to fly to South Vietnam. One more time, Susan had to pack up our household and move, this time back to Oklahoma with her family. At this time, her father was at Tinker Air Force Base in Tulsa, Oklahoma. With me in Vietnam, she would be surrounded by family and have the love and support that she had needed since we were first married. Susan and I took the time to reconnect with her parents, and we put what little furniture and clothing we had in storage, only keeping out what Susan would need to live for the next year. We tried working on our relationship, but it was difficult. The thirty-day leave went by quickly, and then it was time to report to Oakland, California. My chief master sergeant father-in-law arranged for me to get a military hop (flight) from Tinker Air Force Base to Riverside, California, and from there, I caught a Greyhound bus to the Oakland Army Depot.

CHAPTER 7

VIETNAM: DUTY, HONOR, COUNTRY

The drive to Tinker Air Force Base took a little longer than we had planned. By the time that I got to air operations, I was late; my aircraft was on the runway, hot and waiting. I felt like I had really screwed up. Here I was, a second lieutenant, holding up the Air Force. I hopped on the shuttle van to the active runway, jumped out, slung my duffle bag over my shoulder, and ran to the aircraft that was waiting to taxi down the runway. The crew chief who was standing in the door grabbed my duffle as I leaped through the door. Within thirty seconds, I was strapped into my seat, and the plane took off.

After the aircraft reached cruising altitude, the pilot came back to get a cup of coffee and see who had held up the departure. I looked up, and the pilot was a brigadier general, and his co-pilot was a colonel. The general said, "This is the first time I've been held up by a second lieutenant!" All I could say was, "Yes, sir. It won't happen again!" The general laughed and went back to the cockpit. I could tell that I was in for some challenging experiences. After landing, I took the bus to the Oakland Army Depot and reported to the reception station for further processing for shipment to Vietnam. I would be in Oakland for twenty-four hours and before flying to South Vietnam.

The military in-processing was over by 5 p.m., so a fellow second lieutenant and I decided to go downtown for our last night in the United States. We were in uniform, since any civilian clothing was already in our overseas duffle bags, ready for Vietnam.

The next morning, we boarded a military aircraft and flew to Clark Air Force Base in the Philippines. From there, we boarded Air Vietnam, a commercial airline with Vietnamese flight attendants, and flew nonstop to South Vietnam. Upon arrival at the reception center, with my paperwork completed, I was assigned to the 1st Cavalry Division (Airmobile) and sent to An Khe for orientation and initial in-country training. The trip from Pleiku to An Khe was terrifying. We rode in a converted school bus that had wire mesh over the windows. We wouldn't be issued weapons until we completed our one-week, in-country orientation. One night during the week of training that included weapons qualification to intelligence briefings, I could not sleep. Around midnight, the barracks area was attacked by mortar fire. All of us immediately went to the safety of nearby bunkers. "Welcome to South Vietnam!" I was scared to death.

What if I could not do my job and keep my soldiers alive? What if I didn't know what to do? After a couple of nights where I had hand-wringing fear and could not sleep, I realized that something had to change. I prayed to God that, whether or not I took a bullet, everything was in His hands. I let go of my fear so I could do my job. I needed to accomplish the mission while keeping my men alive. When I got to An Khe, my battalion was on palace guard on the rear division headquarters, a posture we'd be in for one week. Palace guard was a term used to identify a unit that was on stand down from combat for a short period. During this time, the battalion could rearm, resupply, and reorganize. The soldiers got a chance to relax for a while. The battalion still had the mission of securing the division rear headquarters from enemy attack. As a second lieutenant in the infantry, I took command of my platoon, which was a forty-man platoon with four squad leaders. Within two days of taking command, I was presented with my first leadership challenge.

Our platoon was to do daytime patrolling in our assigned sector and then at night set up ambush sites. On day three of our patrol, we stopped, set up a perimeter defense, and took a quick lunch by the small river that ran through our sector. Suddenly, I heard a lot of yelling and shouting and hooting and hollering. I went to investigate and saw that across the river, naked Vietnamese women were asking my men to cross over for some "boom-boom." My men started taking off their shirts and pants, ready to cross "the Rhine," but I stopped them. I immediately called an end to the lunch break and had the platoon continue its mission to patrol our sector. The men were angry with at me for not letting them have "a little fun." I knew that the men would be angry, but I knew that many bad things could have happened to my men. I couldn't take the chance. We continued the patrol to end up at our night defensive position.

Later that night, all four squad leaders came to me and asked to talk. Three of them had been in-country, seeing combat for six months or more and were veterans at accomplishing the mission while staying alive. They sat me down and told me that, because of my actions at the river, they trusted that I wanted to maintain discipline and look out for the lives of all the men in the platoon. Specifically, they said, "We will teach you how to accomplish the mission and keep us all alive at the same time." They taught me everything that they had learned over the last six months, and together we began to build the most effective fighting unit in the company. First Platoon, called Whiteskull (the radio call sign for communicating with the company commander or other platoons), became the go-to platoon for all the challenging missions. The company commander had complete confidence that the first platoon would accomplish the most difficult missions. I was very proud of the men, who did everything asked of them.

The company had been conducting intensive daytime patrolling in platoon and squad-sized elements across the Bong Son plains for about three months. The combat patrols were so effective that the Viet Cong and the North Vietnamese Army (NVA) soldiers stopped moving during the day. All enemy movement through our area of operation happened at night. The company commander decided that we would have to conduct night raids to find and destroy the enemy. First Platoon was ordered to train for and conduct the first of these raids. The CO came up with the designation "hunter-killer" teams. I realized that moving at night with a squad-sized unit in absolute silence was demanded. Properly trained, the American soldier can accomplish anything. Conducting a nighttime combat patrol in total silence is not impossible. Whiteskull men learned how to make sure their weapons, equipment, and clothing made no sound while moving.

Each squad would move in total silence, using hand and arm signals to communicate. Because of the effectiveness and cohesion of the men, Whiteskull became the first platoon in the company to do night patrolling. We were known as a "hunter-killer" team. I successfully led the first two "hunter-killer" raids. On September 16, 1967, a Whiteskull squad led by the senior squad leader led a raid during a monsoon rainstorm to locate a suspected small NVA unit moving through our area. The seven-man "hunter-killer" team happened onto a cluster of three small huts. The squad leader began positioning the squad members on each of the four corners of the surrounding area.

As the last of the squad got into position, several NVA soldiers came out of one of the huts, and all hell broke loose. They unleashed machine gun fire, hand grenades, and all types of firepower, which had a devastating effect on the NVA soldiers.

The NVA suffered multiple casualties. At the first volley of fire, the Whiteskull squad leader recognized that they were outnumbered three to one. He called for help. By this time, the rain had increased and visibility was poor. As I got the call from my squad leader, I immediately mobilized a Whiteskull squad and began leading the rescue mission to save the "hunter-killer" team in contact. Moving to the ambush site, we came under heavy fire from the retreating NVA soldiers.

Repelling the attack, we continued to rescue the first squad. Upon arriving and setting up defensive positions, the remaining NVA soldiers attacked again. While fighting off this attack, I located the two wounded squad members and immediately called for a medevac. It was raining so hard that I wasn't sure the helicopter would make it to the makeshift landing zone we had just secured. Standing by the LZ, I got a radio call from the medevac. I couldn't believe it. Despite the worst flying conditions made under enemy fire, the medevac landed and loaded the wounded soldiers on board. There are not enough words of praise to honor those brave pilots flying in South Vietnam. The rest of the squad and I successfully returned to the company without any further enemy contact.

The company found itself in another combat situation on October 20, 1967. We were in a temporary defensive perimeter for a quick lunch break when the perimeter came under heavy and intense enemy fire. I immediately moved from position to position, directing the Whiteskull platoon to return fire. I then led a squad conducting a counterattack and successfully neutralized the enemy with a heavy barrage of suppressive fire. The enemy threat was no more.

Between June 1967 and January 1968, the Whiteskull platoon was so successful in night combat operations that it received accolades from the battalion and brigade commanders. Our platoon continued to be successful during campaigns during Tet in Hue, as well as in Ashau Valley and Khe-Son Valley. The combat experience that I gained from my squad leaders taught me that leadership is about taking care of your men, and, in return, the men will take care of you. It's a lesson that I'll never forget. There were a couple of times when I KNEW God had something greater planned for me, because I had faced combat situations that should have killed me.

After commanding the rifle platoon for more than seven months, I was promoted to first lieutenant and assigned as executive officer for our company. I managed logistics and payroll for the company, frequently flying back and forth from base camp to the jungle. That job was a lot of fun. I enjoyed bringing mail, sodas, food, supplies, and paychecks to the soldiers at least every other day while they trudged through the jungle seeking and destroying the enemy.

Toward the end of April 1968, the commander of a sister company was badly injured and needed to return to the United States. Orders told me to report to the battalion commander immediately, and when I did, he told me he wanted me to take command of the sister company. As a first lieutenant, I knew that captains were standing in line to take command of a company in combat. Commanding a company in combat was a sure ticket to a very successful career in the Army. My ego immediately spoke up, "Yes, sir! I will take the command!"

For the next two and a half months, I commanded the company trying to clear the enemy rocket belt surrounding Camp Evans, the 1st Cavalry Division Forward Base. It was day after day of continually chasing the enemy as they fired 122mm rockets into the division base. The company did everything that it could to find and destroy the enemy. As a company, we did everything we could to minimize casualties. We would move into our night defensive position well after dark and move out the next morning before first light. Still, we would get mortar and rocket attacks during the night. Even with all those defensive tactics, the company suffered casualties. I successfully commanded the company for those months, but my one-year tour-of-duty commitment was fast approaching. That meant it would not be long before I would return to the States.

I had been in command of the company for more than two months, and the battalion commander said that, if I stayed on, I would receive an Officer Efficiency Report for my three months of company command time in combat. I thanked him for his vote of confidence in my leadership ability, but I'd had enough combat and was ready to get home. The next week, I turned command of the company over to a captain and hopped a helicopter to Cam Ranh Bay to begin out-processing to return to the United States. I was excited and relieved to be able to think about coming back home to my family. Out-processing went quickly, and I boarded a Delta jet to fly non-stop to Seattle, Washington.

On the long return flight, I re-lived all the combat experiences that I had in Vietnam. I realized that life is very temporary and could end in an instant. I watched men die, and I knew that I had come close to dying. On that flight home, I made a solemn vow to be the very best husband, father, son, and career officer that I could be. I knew how important every minute of every day was and that I needed to make the most of every opportunity.

When I was in Vietnam, I didn't drink much. Any drinking happened during a twenty-four-hour stand-down and then back into the jungle to search and destroy. I knew that I was capable of not drinking, especially as a lifestyle. Now God had given me a new opportunity, a new chance to do the right thing every day. I was going to take advantage of this opportunity. I had a spiritual experience. Now it was time to go home.

When I left Cam Ranh Bay, I brought home a bolt-action Chinese rifle as a war souvenir. While in combat in the Ashau Valley, we found an NVA supply depot that stored 12,000 Chinese rifles. The brigade commander authorized every soldier in the Brigade the opportunity to take one of these rifles home, and when I landed in Seattle, I had to wait for it to come off the plane. I was the last one at the luggage terminal to get both my duffle bag and my rifle. When they finally arrived, I grabbed my bag, slung the rifle over my shoulder, and proceeded to the ticketing area to book a flight back to Oklahoma.

As I walked down the concourse, it was like I was Moses parting the Red Sea. Everyone waiting for their flights, slammed up both sides of the concourse, possibly out of fear, and shouting unkind words at me. I ignored them all and continued to my next flight. Unsurprisingly, I had no difficulty getting a seat in the waiting area. That experience prepared me for the next few years. I knew that civilians didn't appreciate me very much, but I was proud to have had the opportunity to serve my country.

*August 1967 on Search and
Destroy with Sergeant Joe
Carrazza in Song Re, RVN.*

*October 1967—RVN on
Patrol in Tuy Hoa, Vietnam.*

CHAPTER 8
FINDING JESUS

The flight from Seattle was uneventful, and I safely arrived
in Tulsa, where Susan waited for me. We drove back to
Haskell to spend my thirty-day leave getting acclimated to life in
the United States. The rebuilding of our relationship was hard
for both of us. I had changed, and so had she, but we wanted to
make our marriage work. The long separation and lack of dealing with the death of our son Erik made communication and
relationship-building hard. We worked in earnest to rebuild our
marriage. I was still numb from being in the jungle just a month
earlier, but I wanted to honor my vows and be the best husband
and career officer that I could be.

In August 1968, I received orders to report back to Fort
Benning, Georgia. The Army assigned me to the Company
Tactics Committee of the Army Infantry School. I was designated as the primary instructor for teaching company-level infantry tactics to those going through the Officer Candidate
Program. I was assigned to teach the airmobile operations
and counter-guerilla operations that were happening in South

Vietnam. This assignment showed that God has a sense of humor, because the last thing that I wanted to do was to teach OCS candidates.

Reflecting on that teaching experience, I now realize that I was feeling and thinking through my post-traumatic stress every day as I stood up in front of 200 cadets and told them that, if they didn't stay awake and pay attention in my class, they would die in Vietnam. That single statement got their attention. During each class, I would share personal combat experiences about combat air assaults and securing hot landing zones, as well as how to conduct cordon and search operations to look for the enemy hiding in local villages. Every day, I would come home from teaching all day and needed to relax. I was having difficulty sleeping and struggled to relax.

Remember that vow to be the best husband that I could be? Well, it went right out the window. I began needing a drink to unwind. It wasn't long before I was drinking the way that I did before I joined the Army. Every night and all weekend, I had a drink in my hand. My work life and drinking life were beginning to wear down my relationship with my wife. I knew that we were in trouble. Without knowing it, I began to withdraw emotionally. I built up an invisible wall around my emotions.

In a desperate attempt to save our marriage, Susan suggested that we consider adopting a baby. After the loss of Erik, the doctors told her that she would never get pregnant again. Susan had a job as a legal secretary in a law firm for an attorney who was handling a discreet petition for adoption. She and I talked it over and agreed that giving a child a home would help us rebuild our marriage. On September 14, 1968, we adopted a seven-day-old baby boy whom we named Matthew. We loved little Matthew, and he was the best baby ever. Rarely did he cry or make a fuss. We were blessed to have Matthew. Susan and I both thought, what's so hard about being a parent? Little did we know what was in the immediate future.

About two months later, Susan told me that she was pregnant. What a shock! Her pregnancy put me in a panic. For the next many months, we enjoyed parenting Matthew while I continued to work during the day and drink myself to sleep at night. Our enjoyable parenting experience came to an abrupt halt on July 15, 1969 when Jeffrey was born. Matthew was a gift—happy faces, smiles all day, and a tremendous appetite. Jeffrey was the complete opposite. He was born with the same lung condition that had killed his brother Erik. For two weeks after his birth, Jeffrey was in an incubator receiving oxygen and ultraviolet lighting for his jaundice. I was so worried and brokenhearted. I was so angry with God, asking Him why He would let this happen again.

The difficulty of Jeffrey's birth caused Susan and I to relive Erik's struggle and death. It drove another wedge between us, and my solution was to drink more. By the grace of God, Jeffrey came home, but he had other medical complications that included club feet, severely crossed eyes, and colic. He would cry twenty-four hours a day because of the colic or because he was struggling with his vision or feet. Rarely did he sleep. And hardly did we.

This time was a nightmare for my wife and I. We were at our wit's end and growing farther apart. I used alcohol to numb the emotional pain, and my drinking got worse. We had two babies in diapers, one of whom was in such discomfort that there was no pleasing him. Those early months felt like absolute hell.

Jeffrey's colic went away when he was six months old. What a miracle! Over the next year, he underwent two surgeries to straighten his eyes, and his feet were cast every week to straighten them. Jeffrey never crawled; he would drag his casted feet around the house. He got fast at moving around the house. Even though most of Jeffrey's medical issues were resolved, he still required eye movement training to address dyslexia from the surgery and enable him to see with 20/20 vision. At this point, the boys became the light of my life, although I still had not dealt with my anger over Erik's death. I was drowning in agony and despair, feeling sorry for myself. I continued to self-medicate with alcohol.

A significant change in my military career soon happened; I was promoted to captain and given the Mechanized Infantry Company to command. My stress levels increased dramatically. At this point, I chose to ignore the obvious signs that my marriage was deteriorating. I focused only on commanding the company. I would work long hours, then come home late and immediately retreat to the living room and start drinking.

During this time, a fellow officer regularly talked to me about attending a weekly Bible study in his home. I repeatedly refused to go. After several months, I finally surrendered and agreed to go one time. Susan wouldn't go with me. She was angry and bitter at God for taking her son and did not want any part of religion. I went alone. It was a typical home Bible study led by my friend and his wife. Besides the three of us, there were three other couples in attendance: two who went regularly and one who was traveling through Georgia on their way to Florida to start a couples' Bible study.

The study started with prayer, and then the leader got into the Scriptures for the evening study. About halfway through the evening, the leader asked the visiting couple to share their testimony. Up to this point in the study, the couple had been open, friendly, happy, and laughing, but as they got into their testimony, they shared that their firstborn son had died within hours of being born. They were at peace with their loss and had serenity. I could not believe what I had just heard and didn't understand how they could have peace and serenity about such a horrible loss. They calmly said that they had accepted Jesus Christ as their Lord and Savior, and through that commitment, His love, peace, and serenity helped them have peace and serenity over their loss.

I told them that I was sick and tired of hurting and asked how I could get a relationship with Jesus Christ. The Bible study leader immediately jumped up and asked me to follow him. Then, he shared the sinner's prayer, and I got on my knees and accepted Jesus Christ as my personal Lord and Savior. I instantly felt a peace and serenity wash over me. I experienced something like never before. It was as if the pain in my heart and the fog in my mind had lifted, and I could embrace God's love. For the first time, I felt relief from the agony and despair that I had been living with for so long. My spiritual journey began that night. Only God knew that, on that night, this visiting couple would be in that Bible study, sharing their testimony that ultimately would save my life.

As a new believer with newfound enthusiasm and hope, I started reading the Bible and memorizing scripture. I began leading home Bible studies for couples and teaching Sunday school. I was a Christian on Wednesday and Sunday but an alcoholic for the rest of the week. I had salvation, but I did not turn over total control of my life to Jesus. I accepted Christ Jesus as my Savior. I included lordship in that acceptance but wasn't willing to give up complete control of my life to God. My biggest hangup is that I wanted to keep my mistress, alcohol. I didn't want to give her up. She was always there, gave me what I wanted, and never judged or failed me. I wouldn't quit, I wouldn't surrender. I kept drinking. I could not live without alcohol. I was powerless, and my life was becoming unmanageable.

Somehow, as alcoholics often do, I was able to excel at my job as a company commander while still trying to be a better husband and father. I was better at the former rather than the latter. I had utterly abandoned my vow of being the best father and husband in exchange for alcohol and my career. I thought that I was living my dream of being a great father, loving husband, and having a successful Army career, but in reality, I was dying in the insanity of being consumed by alcoholism. I was living in denial.

The Army recognized my outstanding job as a company commander by issuing orders to send me to the University of

Omaha in Nebraska to complete my bachelor's degree. In the fall of 1970, I once again uprooted my family and moved us all to Omaha. School went well, and my home life got into a routine, but my drinking did not stop. I continued to drink excessively daily, and Susan continued to tolerate me and enable my alcoholic behavior. In June 1971, I graduated with a bachelor's degree in general studies. I received orders to report to Fort Knox, Kentucky, to attend the Armored Officers Advanced Course as an infantry officer.

CHAPTER 9
IF NOTHING CHANGES

Susan and I arrived at Fort Knox and moved into military housing on base. I started attending the armored officer advanced course and adjusted to the new lifestyle. I enjoyed the schooling and social life; my wife and I attended the many parties held for the officers. I was careful to disguise my heavy drinking while at these events. At this point in my drinking, I knew that I was an alcoholic, but I also knew that I could successfully drink while doing a great job at work as well as being a supportive husband. What a delusion. To conceal my alcoholism, I would have two or three drinks at home before the party, then only drink one or two glasses while there. I'd then go home and finish off the night with four or five more drinks. Publicly, I was a responsible drinker, but at home, I was a drunk. I was acting selfish and self-centered, thinking only of myself while drowning my emotions in alcohol. I didn't want to feel. After completing the nine-month advanced course, I was assigned to the Allied Officer Training Department (AOTD) as an instructor at the Armor School, teaching infantry tactics to Cambodian and Laotian officers.

My drinking at home continued to get worse. I came home one day to find a note on the door from Susan. That note said that she was finished and would tell me where to send the furniture. She had packed up her immediate travel needs, and she and my two sons had left for parts unknown. She called me two days later and told me to send all of the household goods to an address in California. I immediately crashed into a feeling of guilt and remorse. I felt utterly alone and that I had lost everything meaningful in my life. Reacting as alcoholics do, those feelings changed to anger and resentment, feeling justified to retaliate. But then I admitted to myself that my alcoholism was the root cause of all my problems. We were divorced six months later. I surrendered all of my rights and didn't contest it. After the divorce, I moved into the substandard bachelor officer's housing on post. The housing allocation funds I received went to my ex-wife as part of the divorce settlement.

This period was the lowest in my life. I had vowed never to be like my parents and get divorced, but there I was. I lived in a one-room billet with an overstuffed chair, a small refrigerator, and a television. I drove a beat-up Ford Falcon that had a broken heater. I was depressed and filled with self-loathing. I felt hopeless and helpless, full of agony and blaming myself. My solution, of course, was to drown my feelings in alcohol. The failure of divorce sent me into a spiral downward into depression, testing my faith. I struggled to focus on God, but alcohol gave me an escape. It was the only way I could deal with the pain of being a failure.

An Airborne position became available in my department, so I asked my commander if I could apply for Airborne School. My request was approved, and I went back to Fort Benning for training. I was hoping to find myself again and reinvent myself. I enjoyed the training except that being the senior captain in the class, I was designated as the student company commander.

That honor caused me to have more attention directed toward my ability to complete the training and command the student company. I finished "jump week" over the Thanksgiving holiday and returned to Fort Knox.

When I got back to Kentucky, I learned that I had been reassigned to be the School Brigade S-4, supply officer. I continued to drink in my off-duty time on nights and weekends. My depression drove me to drink even more. I went on a sick call to see a psychiatrist for counseling. I thought that I was mentally ill and that my solution was to get the psychiatrist to give me a pill to take away the bad feelings. I thought I needed therapy. After a brief assessment, the psychiatrist said I had a choice. I could continue to work, eat, sleep, and drink, or I could take a risk, reach out to trust people and get back into life. I was disappointed with the psychiatrist's assessment. I thought that I needed more help. All he did was tell me to change my lifestyle and trust people. He didn't understand anything about me or my problems. I was desperate, so I decided to take the risk.

I fell back on the spiritual experience that I'd had at Fort Benning and decided to go back to church, teach Sunday school, and sing in the chapel choir. While at Fort Benning, I would be a Christian on Wednesday and Sunday but a drunk the rest of the week. I continued that lifestyle now at Fort Knox, following my spiritual journey while keeping my relationship with my mistress—alcohol. On my first night at choir practice, I saw the choir pianist/organ player, who accompanied the choir, and decided that I wanted to get to know her. She was flirting with one of the members in the choir who was a doctor, and I immediately decided that I didn't stand a chance. I wrote off the possibility of even meeting her, even though she had also attended my Sunday school class.

About this time, one of my work buddies kept telling me that he and his wife knew a great woman who I should get to know, and he wanted to set us up on a blind date. I resisted and said no way. My friend persisted, and I finally agreed to go on this blind date. The night before, I spent a typical Friday hanging out at the Officer Club Annex a block from my living quarters on post. I was sitting at the bar when I saw the church organist walk in with her friend and sit at a corner table. I kept staring at the ladies, and after two more drinks, I worked up the courage to walk over and introduce myself. They invited me to join them, and during our conversation, I learned that the organist, whose name was Shirley, was my blind date! What a surprise! Our date the next night turned into a long and intense relationship over the next few months. Shirley was the second woman in my life to show interest in me, and I fell hard.

CHAPTER 10

A NEW WIFE AND ARMY SUCCESS

My courtship of Shirley was amazing. I was overwhelmed that this woman would love me so completely. Our love continued to blossom as we met for dinner, saw each other Wednesday nights at choir practice, and spent weekends together. The only challenge was winning the acceptance of her two children. Her older daughter readily accepted me, but her younger daughter had some reservations. She told me early on that she didn't want me around and that I was not going to marry her mother. I was sitting on the couch at Shirley's house one evening when the younger daughter snuck up behind me, bit me on the arm, and said, "I don't like you!" I reached back and gently put my mouth on her wrist and said, "You really should not bite people." She was astonished. It turns out, that little episode was our bonding moment. From that point on, we were the closest of friends. My nickname for her became Brat, and I still call her that to this day. Our courtship continued, and I was enjoying every minute with Shirley. I was careful to drink moderately when we were together. Other times, I could continue to drink heavily. I tried to conceal how much alcohol I'd consume each day.

After several months of dating, I realized that Shirley was the one I could spend the rest of my life loving. I was about ready to propose when I received orders to be assigned to the Army Recruiting Command and stationed in Norwalk, Connecticut. I was to report in sixty days after attending sales management training that would prepare me to command a recruiting area in western Connecticut.

I took Shirley to the Officer's Club for dinner and asked her to marry me and, oh, by the way, I'd be leaving in two months. Would you believe that the wonderful lady said yes to my proposal? We worked out the details of me moving to Connecticut and decided that she would join me later. Boy, was I a lucky guy; the happiest on the planet. Two months later, I left for my training and reported to Connecticut. Shortly after arriving in Norwalk, I rented a two-bedroom apartment. I jumped into learning everything I could about enlisting men and women into the now all-volunteer Army. I was working with my master sergeant twelve to eighteen hours a day, because we were both divorced bachelors with only work to occupy our time. We would often work after hours at one of our apartments, discussing recruiting and sharing drinks to pass the time. This habit undoubtedly supported my need for alcohol. We mutually supported each other's addiction to alcohol.

There was just one problem. I was lonely and really missed Shirley. We talked every night, but it wasn't enough. When I could not stand the loneliness any longer, I pleaded with her to come to Connecticut so that we could get married immediately. My two boys were with their mom in California, and her two girls were with her ex-husband in Kentucky. I planned to have the government ship her household goods to Connecticut. Shirley left Kentucky in the middle of December and drove through a terrible snowstorm in New York and Connecticut to get to me. Fortunately, Shirley and her belongings arrived safely. I was in heaven. I had everything that I wanted, a great job, and I was getting married.

I finally felt completely whole. We visited with several pastors to find someone to marry us, but because we were both divorced, the first two pastors would not marry us. Fortunately, we found a pastor from the United Church of Christ to perform the ceremony, and we were married in Milford, Connecticut, on January 24, 1974. The ceremony consisted of the pastor, my master sergeant, and the two of us. A woman from the church arrived just before the ceremony with flowers for my bride. It was a simple but meaningful ceremony.

The next six months were the traditional honeymoon phase of our lives. It was great except that, practically every night, I had to go and meet with my master sergeant to work on changing the culture in the five recruiting stations that we commanded. Those recruiting stations were only reaching 50 percent of their monthly enlistment goal. My master sergeant and I would work late into the evening several times a week, solving issues, and, of course, we were drinking all the time. During those work sessions, I was careful to control the amount of alcohol I drank. I was able to drink a lot while appearing to be under control. I had a high tolerance for alcohol. I think that is where the term "functioning alcoholic" originated.

Shortly after the wedding, Shirley got a job as a nurse at the local Veterans Administration hospital. Our schedules were crazy; I was working long hours, and she was working nights at the hospital. One night, I came home late to find that my wife was not there. It wasn't her night to work late, so I panicked. Where was she? She walked in very upset about an hour later, saying that we needed to talk. I thought she was about to lecture me about my drinking, but Shirley was upset with how much time I spent at work. She said that I wasn't a supportive partner in our marriage. I made a commitment to her that I would cut back on my overtime and believed that I had dodged a bullet, successfully hiding my addiction to alcohol.

About six months after Shirley and I got married, I received a call from Susan, my ex-wife. She said that our two boys were too much of a challenge, and she could no longer care for them. Susan said she was going to put them on the next plane from Los Angeles to Connecticut, and I was to take care of them during the school year while she took them for a month or so in the summer. Matthew and Jeffrey joined us in Connecticut two days later. Our two-bedroom apartment was not too crowded; it was small and cozy.

We all had to adjust, and as a stepmother, Shirley tried to make the best of a new situation in getting to know my boys. Three weeks after my sons arrived, Shirley's ex-husband called to tell her he could no longer handle their two girls, so he was putting them on a plane to Connecticut. After six months of honeymoon bliss, we went from a family of two to a family of six. Talk about a shock. We all continued to adjust to our new family; the four kids got to know each other while Shirley and I tried to manage as parents and stepparents. The two-bedroom apartment was no longer big enough, so we moved into government housing in Milford. The house was small, but it had three bedrooms and two bathrooms.

The boys had their room, and the girls had their room. Shirley and I began to learn how to best manage this "Brady Bunch" family, helping everyone work toward bonding together. The kids started building a strong relationship. We continued to work on discipline issues learning every day about building a family. To help the bonding, we thought adding a dog to the family would bring everyone together. The kids thought it was a great idea. Not thinking this decision through completely, I saw a notice of a family hoping to find a new home for a two-year-old black Great Dane. Loving the breed as much as I did, I jumped on the opportunity and got the dog. The kids welcomed Caesar with enthusiasm, but Shirley was skeptical. It was not long before everyone fell in love with Caesar.

The recruiting stations started to succeed, making 100 percent of their mission each month, and our family began to get into a routine, and I continued to drink every night to "relax." The family of an alcoholic does everything it can to learn how to cope with the chaos caused by the alcoholic's behavior. Often, the family coping skills become unhealthy. The family does what it can to keep the peace. My drinking every night drove the family to develop coping rituals to avoid any conflicts about my drinking. For the next three years, we continued to deal with life challenges with the boys and girls flying back to California and Kentucky during the summer months, and my wife and I working trying to keep everyone growing together. The real challenge was that, as the kids returned from California and Kentucky, we had to re-establish a structure and routine for play, school, and chores. It took time to get everyone on board, having a family of six working together. I typically was physically present but absent emotionally and mentally. I used alcohol to retreat from the chaos. My wife was enjoying her job at the VA, and I continued to be hard at work meeting recruiting goals.

After a very successful assignment in recruiting, the Army rewarded me with the opportunity to attend a master's degree program at Fort Lee, Virginia, at the Army Logistics Management Center. In 1976, our family moved into a townhouse in Petersburg, and the children attended the local public school. The year flew by and, before I knew it, I had graduated with a master's in logistics management. I continued to excel even though I was drinking heavily every day. I continued to drink heavily, and my body increased its tolerance for alcohol. I could drink more and more alcohol without the traditional side effects anyone would recognize as being drunk. I never drank on the job but did before and after work.

Halfway through the school year, the Army promoted me to the rank of major. After I graduated, I received orders to report to the naval base at Norfolk, Virginia, to attend the Armed Forces Staff College, which is the equivalent of the Army's Command and General Staff College. This assignment was an indication that I was on the fast track for future success. Our family moved to Norfolk and settled into another living routine. The family loved being on the naval base because it had a movie theater, a bowling alley, and a base exchange all within walking distance from our housing. The kids had a fun time, and I enjoyed the school while continuing to drink. My wife didn't work because we were only going to be stationed there for nine months. It was an excellent time for the family, and we spent a lot of time together. Still, while I was physically present, I was mentally and emotionally absent because of my drinking. I would come home from work and immediately start drinking. I would sit in front of the television and drink one beer after another. I was more interested in drinking than interacting with Shirley and the kids.

Upon completion of the Staff College in 1978, I received orders to Nuremberg, Germany, assigned to the 1st Armored Division as the operations officer for the Division Support Command. I flew to Germany ahead of my family so I could go through in-processing reporting to the Division and get on the list for military housing in Nuremberg. Within a month, I had received military housing, and my family joined me in Germany. The move was not without its challenges. I'm in Germany, starting my new job while Shirley had to deal with all the packing and taking care of the kids and Caesar. Packing up our life in Virginia was no easy task and had to be done in two shipments. The first small shipment contained all the things needed for living in the short term. That shipment would arrive at the same time the family arrived in Germany. The second, larger shipment containing all the remaining household would arrive by boat about sixty days later. I didn't realize that there would be a problem flying Caesar to Germany. My wife had to find someone to build a shipping crate six-feet long, two-feet wide, and five-feet high to accommodate Caesar. You could say that Caesar had an exciting trip flying to Germany in the belly of a cargo jet. Once our car and household goods arrived, we were in business. The kids enrolled in the Department of Defense school, and Shirley got a job as the school nurse. It was a great learning experience for the kids, but my wife had difficulty adjusting to the German culture. I worked long hours and spent a lot of time in the field doing combat exercises.

The one blessing during those three years was that we were able to take one week each year as a family and go to one of the Armed Forces Recreation Areas: Chiemsee, Berchtesgaden, and Garmish. We went to a different area each year, and the kids learned how to ski. They still talk about their skiing experiences to this day. After six months of living in government housing in Nuremberg, we moved into a massive mansion in the downtown area. The kids got to play with other German kids, and they got very proficient in speaking the language. We all loved living "on the economy," and I liked the house and its location because I could walk one block to the local gasthouse to drink and not have to drive home. I became great friends with many of the locals who came to the gasthouse. It was great. It was heaven. The more alcohol that I drank at the gasthouse, the better my German got. Many nights, the elder German drinking buddies would walk me home. I was even able to have the local beer distributor deliver cases of beer to our house every week. The family was indifferent about the beer deliveries. It was just another typical dysfunctional family coping behavior, "keep the alcoholic happy."

I had a successful experience as the operations officer for the support command, but my real desire was to be an executive officer for an infantry battalion in Germany. I submitted my request for an assignment to an infantry battalion and received orders to go to Crailsheim, Germany. I was to report to be the executive officer of the 1st Battalion 51st Mechanized Infantry Battalion. This assignment was my dream, propelling me up through the ranks to be a battalion commander and then a general officer. I was continuing to be a successful career officer. My family joined me, and we lived in the military barracks on the Kaserne in Crailsheim.

This assignment was challenging because I found myself in the middle of the tension between the battalion commander and the four company commanders. The tension became evident when the battalion underwent a series of division-level maintenance inspections of all the equipment. It was my responsibility to ensure that the battalion passed all the inspections. Because of this tension between the battalion commander and company commanders, it was challenging to motivate the company commanders to have their soldiers work long hours to get ready for these inspections—the result: multiple inspection failures. I failed to accomplish my duty and let the battalion down. It was a low point in my military career. I felt ashamed and like a complete failure. I thought my successful military career was over because this less than outstanding efficiency report would kill any future success. I fell back into feeling hopeless and helpless.

I did find a lot of solace in drinking during my three years in Germany. Each year there were training exercises of two to three months in length. I never drank during these field exercises; that was my way of showing everyone that I was not an alcoholic since a real alcoholic could not quit for any length of time.

Following my dismal assignment as a battalion executive officer, I received orders in 1981 to report to the 2nd ROTC Command at Fort Knox. This news made Shirley, the kids, and Caesar very happy. For the family, it meant going back home to Radcliff, Kentucky. They would reunite with grandparents and familiar surroundings. We all settled into family housing on post, and my wife got a nursing job at the hospital at Fort Knox. My assignment was to Camps Division, which ran the summer basic camp for all college students who wanted to join ROTC in their junior year. These students had to complete the six-week basic camp at Fort Knox to be eligible to enroll in ROTC at their university in the fall. Our division ran the summer-long basic training camp for the cadets. The kids settled in once again, and my wife enjoyed working at the hospital. I enjoyed helping run the camp for 6,000 cadets every summer. This job was very demanding, and I spent a lot of time in the field, making sure that training was effective. Running the camp was very complicated. The cadre was responsible for receiving 300 cadets each week for each class, getting them issued clothing and field gear, and assigning them to a barracks. The cadre ensured professionally conducted training. I was responsible for overseeing all aspects of the cadet experience, which included a protocol branch that greeted and escorted VIP visitors and college ROTC staff around the camp to monitor the training of their cadets. The job was challenging and fun. I thrived on seeing cadets complete the camp training.

Promoted by Col. Wilkerson and Jay's wife, Shirley.

Receiving a recruiting award from Colonel Falberg.

The Davidson family at the promotion ceremony.

CHAPTER 11

ALCOHOL TAKES ITS TOLL

The commanding general of the 2nd ROTC Region ran a tight ship. Colonels, lieutenant colonels, majors, and captains made up the majority of the organization, along with a few non-commissioned offers. The general and sergeant major led physical training three days a week. In bad weather, exercises happened in the nearest gymnasium. From my perspective, things could not get any better. Running the camp was great, but I continued to drink myself to sleep every night. I returned to the state of being physically present but emotionally and mentally absent. The kids were in school, and my wife was working at the hospital. The Army notified me that I was selected for promotion to lieutenant colonel with the date of rank to be determined when Congress passed a bill with my sequence number attached to the legislation. All I had to do was continue impressing everyone on the job and taking care of my family. I believed that I had everyone convinced I was an outstanding soldier and a great husband and father. Once again, I was living in delusion.

My sons had returned from their summer in California and started the school routine. After a couple of months, Jeffrey could no longer keep a secret and told me that he and Matthew had worked out a plan with their mom that when they went back to California the next summer, they would stay there and live with her. The boys were now both thirteen years old, and they decided that they were old enough to choose where they wanted to live. I was angry at my ex-wife for manipulating my sons to come live with her behind my back. I knew it had nothing to do with my alcoholic behavior, which she had dealt with for nineteen years, mostly long-distance. I blamed my ex-wife for being selfish, thinking only of herself. I got drunk that night. The next day I got angry with the boys and told them that, if living with their mom was what they wanted, then they could leave for California right away. Typical alcoholic thinking. It hurt that the boys would rather live in California with their mother than live with me. I couldn't take the painful feeling of abandonment, so I self-medicated with alcohol. The boys left, and I continued to work at the camp, monitoring training and greeting VIP visitors from colleges across the country.

At this point in my drinking career, I continued to drink almost entirely at home to keep precisely how much I drank a secret from everyone except for my wife and daughters. I made one of those alcoholic decisions to show everyone that I'm not an alcoholic, and I switched from distilled spirits to beer. The only problem with that decision was that I was still drinking the same amount of alcohol every night.

It was now 5 a.m. on a Wednesday, and I had overslept because I had drunk nearly a case of beer the night before. The liver can only process one ounce of alcohol per hour; so at 5 a.m., I was still drunk. I hopped in the car and drove to the Field House, where the general and the sergeant major were conducting physical training. I got to the parking lot, and I was late. I had to park a distance away from the Field House, so I started to run, dressed in my running suit and tennis shoes. Halfway to the Field House, both feet tripped over one of those curbs in the parking lot, and I fell forward—catching myself with the palms of both hands and both knees as I hit the pavement. I tore holes in my running suit and was bleeding from both knees and hands. I was still so drunk that I didn't feel any pain. That might have been shocking; I don't know.

I got up and tried to sneak into the physical training that had already started. I attempted to hide in the back of the formation and hoped that no one noticed that I was bleeding or that my running suit was torn. After exercising, my boss, a lieutenant colonel, told me to go home and get cleaned up before coming back to the training camp. No one else said anything about my grand entrance, so I figured I had fooled everyone. I was home free once again! What crazy thinking. That's typical of an alcoholic.

That is when the proverbial s*** hit the fan. It was 6 a.m. on Monday, February 7, 1983, when I entered my office at Camps Division, and I saw my immediate supervisor, who was never in the office before 10 a.m., sitting at my desk. This became "**My Darkest Hour**":

> *The general says that if you don't get a handle on your alcoholism, he will kick you out of the Army in forty-five days!*

As I wrote earlier, I had asked Shirley to call and get me into treatment. After several calls, she realized that I was the one who had to make those calls. I finally concluded that the only acceptable course of treatment that would satisfy the commander was to enter the intensive outpatient program at Fort Knox's Community Counseling Center.

February 9, 1983, is when I began my journey of recovery from addiction to alcohol.

I was so afraid and scared. Feeling hopeless and helpless, I reached out to God as I had when I came to terms with the death of my firstborn son. I hit my knees, and humbly asked God to do for me what I could not do for myself: stop drinking. I had turned my will and my life over to God back in August 1969. I had accepted God's salvation and turned over everything in my life to Him except my drinking. Now I admitted that I was powerless over alcohol, and my life had become unmanageable. Alone, in the quiet of my bedroom, crying so hard that I was shaking, I prayed, telling God that I could not stop drinking without HIM. I asked God to do for me what I could not do for myself. I confessed that I was selfish and self-centered, having accepted God's grace of salvation but refusing to surrender to the lordship of God. I now realized that I needed to end my relationship with my mistress—alcohol. For the first time in my life, I completely surrendered to the God of my understanding.

Alcohol had been my mistress. She was ever faithful, always present, never said no, and always made me feel good. I knew my mistress had to die, so I began the grieving process. I went through all of the phases of grief. I looked back and saw my life full of insane behavior. I now understood what lordship meant—turning away from self-will and being committed to seeking God's will. I deeply reconnected with God; I felt safe, secure, and wrapped in the warmth of God's love for really the first time in my life. I felt unconditional love without expectation. Going through alcohol addiction treatment at Fort Knox while on active duty was a humbling experience for me. I learned what it meant to surrender and truly be humble. I attended my daily group sessions in uniform, along with all the enlisted soldiers.

I honestly had to surrender my ego. At the direction of my clinical therapist and the mandatory part of the intensive out-patient treatment program, I had to attend the local Alcoholics Anonymous meeting. I drove myself to my first meeting. I knew how to follow directions even reluctantly. I was fearful of being judged and being rejected. During that very first AA meeting, I experienced acceptance and understanding from my fellow alcoholics. I remember that first Alcoholics Anonymous meeting, sitting at a long table as everyone began introducing themselves in the traditional AA manner. They would say, "Hello, I'm John, and I am an alcoholic." I sat at the table, my knees bouncing up and down so hard I was shaking it and rattling all of the metal ashtrays. When it became my turn, I whispered, "I'm Jay, an alcoholic." They said to speak louder because they couldn't hear me. It took two more times before my introduction was loud enough for all to hear. Their immediate response was, "We love you and keep coming back!"

I was so overwhelmed with unconditional love. I had never experienced anything like this because I thought the real Jay deep inside was unlovable. And unwanted. That's what my life experience had taught me. Here, four men and women were saying that they loved me with no expectations and that they knew me as an alcoholic. What a relief! What a feeling of new possibilities of a new life without alcohol. What a gift I received that night, a gift that was freely given. I was overwhelmed with a feeling of being needed and loved. That gift has continued to be given to me every day of my sobriety.

Left to right—Brigadier General Lightner and Brigadier General Isaac Smith with Jay's father-in-law in the background.

Jay promoted to lieutenant colonel by Brigadier General Isaac Smith.

CHAPTER 12

DARKEST HOUR— LOSING A DREAM COME TRUE

The gift that the AA group gave me was total and complete unconditional love. It was and is a love that I had been looking for all my life, even though I thought alcohol was my solution. This newfound love gave me courage for the first time in my life to face reality without alcohol. It was a spiritual awakening like what I had experienced back in 1969, but now it was so totally consuming me with love and peace. I could and did grieve the death of my mistress. I gave up all reservations and completely surrendered my will and my life over to God as I understood him.

With that final act, I began to realize what lordship truly meant and was able to surrender myself to a power greater than myself completely. It was a significant turning point in my relationship with God. God now became the center of my universe, and I began studying the Bible in earnest, even memorizing scripture. I learned how to lead Bible studies and lead people to salvation. I learned how to love myself. I learned how to share unconditional love in the AA fellowship, at church, and on the job, running the ROTC basic camp each year. I had a great clinical therapist who helped me deal with my demons. My therapist was a good listener. I talked about my lifelong belief that I was less than and suffered a fear of rejection. The therapist was skilled in helping me recognize that I was successful and should be proud of my accomplishments.

At an early age, I learned that love could often hurt, so for protection, I put a wall around my heart. I began trying to please people to keep from being hurt. One of the most beautiful blessings from the recovery fellowship is the constant and consistent unconditional love without expectation. Experience had taught me that love always costs. My brothers and sisters in the recovery fellowship gave me love and acceptance and the AA fellowship, which gave me the opportunity to share unconditional love. After four months of intensive outpatient therapy, the commanding general of the 2nd ROTC Region promoted me to lieutenant colonel on June 15, 1983. By the grace of God, my dream had come true.

My family was so happy that I had found the solution. On one occasion, Shirley and I decided to go to the Kentucky State Fair in Louisville. She was longtime friends with the owners of the midway carnival that had all the concession rights during the ten-day event. When we got to the midway, we went to the office trailer where her friends met us. It was the last Saturday of the fair, and the owner asked me if I would like to help them because there was so much to do to close everything up. I was thrilled. My job was to take a five-gallon black trash bag and visit all twenty ticket booths to collect the cash, because it wasn't a good idea to let too much money accumulate at each booth. It took me one hour to visit all twenty booths. I asked the owner what I could do next, and he told me to make another round.

Five hours and five trips later, the show closed, and the midway shut down. The whole scene was exhilarating. My adrenalin was pumping. What a lifestyle! What fun! My wife and I spent the next five hours sorting, stacking and counting the money preparing it for the bank deposit. It was now 6 a.m. on Sunday, and the ride operators were all loaded up and ready to drive to the next town to set up the rides for the next show. My wife and I had the time of our lives, and it was a night that we would never forget.

One of the blessings that came out of all of my struggles with alcohol and the embarrassment I endured was that I completed intensive outpatient treatment and continue to be successful as chief of staff for the ROTC basic camp. The general who vowed to kick me out of the Army if I did not get a handle on my alcoholism was the same general that promoted me to lieutenant colonel on June 15, 1983. God answers prayers. I was living my childhood dream of serving in the US Army and being promoted to lieutenant colonel.

I continued as chief of Camps Division for the next few months, awaiting new orders as I had finished the standard three-year assignment. The Army told me that my medical record was sealed, and my treatment for alcoholism would not be in my formal military record, but I didn't believe it. I just knew that my military career was over. I finally received my orders and found out that I was going to Washington, DC, I could not believe my eyes. I thought that I would go to the Pentagon, which would be the best assignment in the world. Reading on, I realized that I wasn't going to the Pentagon—I was going to the Army Material Command (AMC) in Alexandria, Virginia. That news burst my bubble. Why didn't I get to go to the Pentagon? A Pentagon assignment would have been a sign that I was on the path toward a battalion command slot. I interpreted that the assignment to AMC was less prestigious than going to the Pentagon, and that battalion command was not to be in the future. My other area of expertise was in logistics, so this assignment to AMC was a utilization assignment.

In August 1983, Shirley and I relocated to Alexandria and moved into a two-bedroom condo. Our children remained with our exes in California and Kentucky. I began working at AMC and immediately felt like a fish out of water. Ninety percent of the military staff at AMC were non-combat arms and took pleasure in reminding me that logistics sustained the battlefield, and I needed to be humble. I worked on that humility daily. I had a history of being able to come into an organization or job that was in trouble and fix the problems that existed. The leadership took advantage of my skills, and I moved from one position to the next over the next three years. I managed the entire Army budget line for anything that had wheels, then anything requiring water or petroleum, and finally anything for the individual soldier. My time at AMC was productive, but I always felt out of place. I was successful in getting great reviews, but I didn't feel like I was a part of the organization. The one thing that kept my life together during this transition was my fellowship with men and women in recovery. I began working the steps again with my sponsor and attending weekly meetings. I frequently called my sponsor to relieve my frustration at work. I felt more a part of the recovery community than part of the Army.

In my third year on assignment at AMC, the owner of the carnival called me out of the blue and made me an offer that I could not refuse. He wanted me to come and join the carnival and learn the business from the bottom up, so that I would be able to take a smaller show on the road. At this point, I was not very satisfied with my job in the Army, so this offer appealed to me. By this time, I was convinced that my military career was over, and that future promotions and exciting assignments were out of the question. Even though I had been awarded the Silver Star and Bronze Star for valor as a Second Lieutenant and had outstanding efficiency reports (except that one from Germany), I knew that my alcoholism had ended my military career.

I remembered the night that Shirley and I had helped close out the Kentucky State Fair and how exciting that was. I saw the carnival as an extension of my military career. It was similar to an infantry battalion, just on a smaller scale. The carnival had its own mess hall, maintenance, transportation, electrical power uniform code, and chain of command. Best of all, it had a complete cadre of workers. I went home to discuss this job offer with my wife, and she already knew all about it. She was excited and supportive. The more we talked about a career change, the more sense it made for me to retire and join the carnival. I think that I was being spiteful, wanting to show the Army that I could command a battalion, even if it were a carnival.

I had completed the required three years serving the grade of lieutenant colonel, allowing me to retire at that grade. The next day, I told the AMC command that I was submitting my retirement request. They were pretty shocked—first, that I was retiring, and second, that I was retiring so that I could join the carnival. They eventually accepted my decision with good humor. At my retirement party, they gave me a cake decorated in a carnival theme. In May 1986, I retired with full military honors at a ceremony and parade conducted by the 3rd Infantry Regiment ceremonial Old Guard at Fort Meyer, Virginia. I was blessed and honored to be able to participate in the ceremony, which marked the end of a very successful military career.

I am grateful to this day for all the experience and rewards that I enjoyed while serving my country for twenty years, but now it was time to learn how to work as a civilian.

May 1986—Jay's retirement ceremony at Fort Meyer,
Virginia, conducted by 3rd IN, The Old Guard.

CHAPTER 13

RETIRING TO JOIN THE CARNIVAL

After twenty years in the Army, I stepped out of my comfort zone to begin a new life as a carnival worker. Where do you even start? Well, my first task was to buy an RV—something I had never owned and knew nothing about. The carnival owner said that they had an RV waiting for us and that I could buy it for a very reasonable price. We were suddenly proud owners of a forty-foot, fifth-wheel RV. I had never towed anything in my life, but there I was, getting ready to drag this monster all over the southeastern United States. There was only one problem. I didn't have a truck to tow the RV. I knew virtually nothing about big trucks, but I found one in Texas that was within our budget. Now we were ready to rock and roll. My wife and I joined the carnival in Alabama, and I began my new career. My job was to learn the carnival business, and my wife worked as a ticket booth operator, selling tickets and armbands to carnival-goers.

My first experience was learning how to set up the carnival
lot. There are methods and reasons for positioning every ride,
food booth, and game on the lot, mostly to maximize the opportunity for visitors to see every ride, eat at every food booth, and
play all the games so that they spend all their money.

Traditionally, at the main entrance of the midway, the carou-
sel is located to welcome the carnival-goers. The best adult ride
goes in the farthest back corner of the lot, while the children's
rides are near the back of the lot as well. This setup encourages
the visitors to walk the entire lot, increasing the probability of
them playing some of the games and buying food.

After I helped to supervise the setting up of the rides, my job
was to work in the office trailer managing payroll, issue the cash
drawers to the ticket booth staff in the evenings, and balance
the cash drawers and make up the cash deposits for the bank at
the end of the night. I completed this routine every night of the
show, which traditionally ran from Thursday through Saturday.
Saturday night was the big night, because armbands were sold
for $5, allowing visitors to ride as many times as they could
tolerate. The show would usually close around midnight or 1
a.m., and the ride crew and maintenance would begin breaking
down the midway in preparation for the jump (move) to the next
town. All the rides would come down, as well as the mess hall
and sleeping quarters for the workers.

At some point during the week, it was my responsibility to
run a route reconnaissance to the next town for the upcoming
show. I would then prepare multiple strip maps for every driver
to follow to ensure they all made it safely. On one of the jumps
to the next town in Eastern Kentucky, I noticed that the tem-
perature gauge on my truck was rising. We were continually going up and downhill, so I didn't think anything about it. That's
when the carnival owner pulled up alongside my truck, yelling
that the truck was on fire! I pulled over, and sure enough, the
engine compartment was on fire. It turns out the transmission
overheated. How was I to know that when hauling a heavy load

such as a forty-foot, fifth- wheel RV that the tow vehicle needed a transmission cooler? We were towed to the town where the carnival was happening, and the truck went to the dealership for repairs. There, mechanics installed a transmission cooler and rewired the engine compartment's electrical system. It was just another life lesson on the road of a carnie.

Shirley and I got comfortable moving every seven to ten days to a new town for their county fair. By Sunday of every jump, the carnival rides, games, and food joints were set up and ready for the state safety inspector to come and inspect. Mondays, Tuesdays, and Wednesdays were the days for maintenance, painting, and repairs to rides. I took the opportunity to get to know the ride operators, or ride jocks. Every day, I would have the time to get to know them. We would broadcast church music and AA speaker tapes during the day. I took every opportunity to share my experience, strength, and hope with the men as they worked repairing their rides. I identified with them. They were my soldiers.

At this point, I was three years sober and making AA meetings in many of the towns where the carnival set up. I was having the time of my life learning the carnival business and relating to the ride jocks. It only took a couple of months before the ride jocks started calling me boss, except there was only one boss on the midway, and it wasn't me. Because our wives were best friends, the owner didn't want to fire me, so he took a different tactic. In addition to all my other duties, he put me in charge of setting up, running, and tearing down one of the children's rides on the midway—Raiders of the Lost Ark. It was the most difficult ride of all, because it used more cotter pins than any other ride and took longer to set up and take down. It was a difficult ride to operate, since you could only have fifteen kids on the ride at any one time. Because of the tunnels and webbing, you could not always see all of the children. Even in sobriety, my alcoholic ego kicked in, and I decided that I would master operating this ride. I would learn how to set the ride up and take it down faster than any other ride on the midway.

After about three weeks of practice and operating the ride, I accomplished my goal. I had this ride up faster than anyone else and was able to take it down just as quickly. My actions only frustrated the owner even more. He thought that I would quit, but I had never quit a job in my life, and I was not going to start now. In September 1986, I had just pulled our truck and RV into a position to set up for the week at the fairgrounds in Huntsville, Alabama. The owner came to me and said, "You're fired. Pull your rig off the midway and go home." My wife and I looked at each other speechless. Fortunately, I was strong enough in my sobriety that I responded rather than reacting as I would have in my alcoholism. We knew that God had a plan. We just didn't know what it was. My wife and I calmly packed up and moved to the nearest motel to begin figuring out what to do next. After a day of looking, I found an RV dealership in Florida that would come and get the RV, take it back, and sell it. Two days later, the RV was gone. I got in my truck, my wife drove in her car with the cats, and we hit the road back to Kentucky to start our life all over again. I now held the dubious distinction of being the only carnie to be fired from the carnival. Another chapter in my life was closed, and a new adventure was about to begin.

CHAPTER 14

WHAT COMES NEXT

A fter leaving the carnival, we arrived in my wife's hometown of Radcliff, Kentucky. We found an apartment to rent and reconnected with my wife's parents. I began looking for a job, but it was a challenge. Everywhere I interviewed, the response was, "You're overqualified. Why do you want to do this type of work?" My answer was that I needed to work to pay bills. About this time, my daughter started dating a young man who was in the process of buying a real estate franchise. Her boyfriend contacted me and asked me if I was interested in joining him in the real estate business. He hired me to manage the company's property management account. My lingering alcoholic ego again kicked in, and I promptly said yes to his offer. Still in early sobriety, I was struggling with my self-will versus God's will. Sure, I didn't know anything about property management, but with my logistics background, how hard could it be? Right? I immediately assumed responsibility for more than 425 properties, including mobile home parks, single homes, and multiplex apartments. What a challenge! I spent 50 percent of my time with the 10 percent of owners who demanded special care and support. I spent 50 percent of my time dealing with irresponsible tenants who managed to damage or destroy the rental property. I learned a lot about stress management. It was a challenging job.

Fortunately, I was back home where I got sober, so I was able to reconnect with my original support group and sponsor. Working with my sponsor, I continued to take a daily personal inventory, and when I realized that I was wrong, I promptly admitted it. This inventory included positive experiences of the day. It was an opportunity to feel and express gratitude for what God was working in my life. Attending hometown AA meetings again was a lifesaver. That unconditional love kept me grounded and focused on seeking God's will for my life. Getting experience in handling property management issues gave me an appreciation for all those managers in the world who do similarly challenging jobs. I took this opportunity to take the real estate course and became a licensed realtor in November 1986. Through all this chaos and turmoil, I was able to achieve a 92 percent occupancy rate of all the rental properties.

Just before I retired from the Army, I had submitted paperwork to volunteer as a retiree to work as a military advisor anywhere in the world where the Army had a mission. In January 1987, I was contacted by the Raytheon Corporation, inquiring about my interest in working with the logistics department of the Royal Saudi Air Defense Force in Riyadh, Saudi Arabia. I flew to Raytheon's corporate office in Andover, Massachusetts, to be interviewed by a Saudi staff officer. That interview did not go well. The Saudi officer was arrogant, demeaning, and very unprofessional. I left Andover feeling that I did not want any part of working with that officer or his staff.

I went back to work in Radcliff, managing properties and enjoying my network of recovery friends. The fellowship was crucial to my sobriety. Shirley and I decided that we needed to get out of renting and build a home. So, we found a parcel of farmland that was being developed for a subdivision, and our house became the first house built in that subdivision. After we moved in, Shirley began to experience strange feelings when she was home alone in the new house. We soon learned that we had built the house near a Native American burial site and needed to make peace with the spirits. Shirley researched how to resolve these strange feelings. We sought the help of a local pastor to come and pray with us to make peace and bless our home. Shirley didn't experience any strange feelings after the pastor's help.

In November 1987, Raytheon contacted me again and asked me to reconsider the logistics advisor position in Saudi Arabia. They were having difficulty finding someone to fill that position. Once again, I traveled to Andover for an interview with a Saudi officer. This interview went much better, and I felt that I could work with him and his staff.

My family obligations and challenges had changed considerably. My mother had passed away from COPD, and my wife had adjusted to the idea of my being away for two years with home visits every six months. I decided to take the job with the understanding that, after six months, my wife would be able to join me in Saudi Arabia. I left for Riyadh in January 1988. While in the military, I had several intercontinental fight experiences, but a fourteen-hour nonstop flight from New York to Jeddah, Saudi Arabia, was a new experience. Once I got to Riyadh, the Raytheon staff welcomed me and I learned that I would share a vehicle and a villa with my new co-worker, who was a retired US Army colonel from the Quartermaster Corps. I thought it was great! I would get to work with an officer who had a logistics background just like the officers I had served with at the Army Materiel Command. But, as an infantry officer, I remembered my difficult interactions with fellow logistics officers, especially full colonels. Because they presumed I had little experience in logistics, I believed that it would be a difficult partnership in addition to living in Saudi Arabia.

I knew this was going to be a difficult two years. The colonel was a knowledgeable but humble person, and we were able to build a great relationship of partnership and friendship. Our only source of information about the United States was the English-only newspaper in Riyadh that was printed once a week. The colonel was an avid baseball fan, and he made me take an oath never to divulge a baseball score before he had a chance to read it in the paper. I did it once, not thinking and was severely chastised. Other than that episode, we had a great relationship.

Our villa was on the edge of town and owned by one of the Saudi princes. It was huge! It had eight bedrooms, five bathrooms, a large dining hall, two large meeting rooms, a front entrance for men, and a side entrance for women. Marble made up the entire interior of the villa. It was indeed a mansion, which was surrounded by a twelve-foot brick wall for security and seclusion. I found out that the reason the wall was twelve feet high was that it prevented someone who was riding a camel from looking over the wall to see the women in the courtyard.

It didn't take me long to get into a routine of driving to the Riyadh Airbase to work for the Office of Defense Logistics for the Royal Saudi Air Defense Force. My typical work week was Saturday through Wednesday, from 9 a.m. until 2 p.m. I was asked to write operations war plans to mobilize, transport, sustain, and maintain the Saudi missile battalions during the war. I wrote these plans in English, and two Sudanese translators would translate them into Arabic. It was a slow process, but the Saudi officers were not in any hurry to have them completed. I used my military experience to plan for load plans, resupply routes, and maintenance during combat operations. Because of prayer calls and the morning and afternoon meals, I spent two or three hours a day writing these plans. After work, my coworker and I would go back to our villa, fix dinner, then go for an hour-long walk in the desert. My partner and I would walk through the neighborhood, looking at all the villas and mosques. We walked long enough to reach the outskirts of town.

We walked into the nearby desert hills. It's difficult to describe, but with no street lights, the desert was dark, and once in the darkness and silence, there was an eerie feeling. We were the only crazy people wandering in the desert.

The nights and weekends were long and empty. I was able to attend an AA meeting at the American Red Cross twice a month, but I was starving spiritually. I started a serious self-directed Bible study picking a word and tracing it through every book and chapter in the Bible, writing a synopsis of what I understood about that word. I would write all this down then mail it to my wife, who was not as enthusiastic about the study as I was. The study of my two favorite books, the Bible and the *Big Book*, helped my sanity in this barren land. Because of my military experience, I was not allowed to travel outside the city limits of Riyadh. That contributed to the empty feeling of long weekends.

Because of the cost, I only called home once a week. During one of the calls, I asked my wife to contact the Officer's Christian Fellowship to see when the US Air Force stationed at the American side of the Riyadh Airbase would have a visit by the Air Force chaplain. I learned that the chaplain would be at the Airbase in one month, and I made the necessary contacts to get permission to go on the United State's side of the base to be able to attend the church service. I was so excited to be able to go to church. When I arrived, there were three others in attendance. After the service, I met a fellow Christian who was a Southern Baptist preacher from California who was in Riyadh to teach English to the Saudi military. Pastor Woody was tithing back to his church in southern California. We formed a Paul-Timothy relationship, and he began to minister to me. This relationship allowed me to grow spiritually like never before. I use the relationship of the disciple Paul and Timothy, his brother in Christ, as an example of our relationship, as noted in 1 Timothy 4:12–16:

Paul, a Disciple of Christ Jesus, is a mentor and spiritual guide to Timothy, his brother in Christ. Paul encouraged Timothy to speak boldly and train himself to be godly. Paul recommended three activities that Timothy should do: first is a public reading of the Scriptures, out of this would flow preaching followed by teaching. Paul exhorted Timothy not to neglect his gift but be diligent in these matters and give yourself wholly to them. (Paraphrase mine.)

This mentoring, fellowship, and learning relationship was an answer to my prayers, allowing me to ask for spiritual guidance and support while endeavoring to remain positive in this desert land.

Pastor Woody had learned that in each of the several housing compounds designated for all non-Saudi contract workers, families were willing to hold secret Bible studies during the week. These families were also providing space for a weekly praise and worship service every Friday. What courageous families they were. Imagine living in an 1,800-square-foot, three-bedroom, ranch-style home and hosting a Friday worship service for seventy-five people. Of course, everyone had to spread out when it came to parking so that the house church would receive no unwanted attention. Everyone carried their Bible hidden and moved in small groups. The praise and worship service was lay-lead and lasted around two hours. There was singing, praises, and a short message from a layperson.

Everyone focused on the unity of spirit. In a time of spiritual adversity, believers from all faiths and denominations came together in total unity. If you had differing religious practices, those happened before or after the worship service. Every denomination worshiped together in one Spirit. The church thrives under persecution. In Saudi Arabia, the practice of the Christian faith is forbidden. Such practice is punishable by imprisonment. All Christian literature, including the Bible, is prohibited and immediately confiscated if found. Anyone caught practicing their Christian faith would be put in prison or deported. One of the biggest challenges was to find Christians that were willing to meet to practice their faith secretly. Most were afraid to identify themselves as Christian believers for fear of deportation. During one of my calls to Shirley, I expressed our frustration at not being able to meet fellow Christians. Shirley reminded me that there were youth swim clubs in each of the international housing compounds. Her idea was to send me Christian fish pins that everyone could wear on their Arabic ID badge. If asked what the pin was, the reply would be for showing support for the youth swim club. This simple sign became the way Christians wanting to practice their faith would find fellow believers. Under this threat of persecution, the Christian faithful in Riyadh gathered in secret in these homes to attend lay-led praise and worship services. Pastor Woody and I would go from one house church to the next each week, ministering as best as we could. We also attended various weeknight Bible studies. It seemed that if we did not practice out in the open, the Saudi religious police left us alone. The house churches banded together and pooled resources. I will never forget the two Easter sunrise services held out in the middle of the desert far away from town. More than one hundred Christians celebrated the resurrection of Christ Jesus. The fellowship and love were powerful. In Riyadh, there was a sizable Filipino population of workers doing the manual labor and city sanitation. The Filipino people are faithfully religious and, despite Saudi persecution, would hold worship services in their homes in the city. The Saudi religious police would arrest the pastor/priest and close the house church. The pastor/priest would be held in prison indefinitely. If someone paid to fly the pastor/priest back to Manila, the pastor/priest would be released to go back to Manila. Our house churches began providing airline tickets to every pastor arrested. What a blessing it was to see these men of God getting freedom.

This ministry to the house churches, and my daily Bible research proved to be my salvation and helped preserve my sanity. The spiritual highlight during my two years in Saudi Arabia were the two Easter Sunday sunrise services in the middle of the Saudi desert. Those services actually happened on a Friday. I helped organize car routes from multiple directions to converge on a single wadi (ravine) to gather and participate in the service. About one hundred people were there. It was truly inspirational.

Six months into my first year in Saudi Arabia, I finally received permission to have my wife join me. I completed all the necessary paperwork, and Shirley was about to make her travel arrangements when she learned that her mother had colon cancer. This event changed all our plans. Shirley stayed in Kentucky to take care of her mother while I continued to write operations plans for the Saudi military during the day. This separation was challenging and became even more difficult when my wife had to stay home to care for her mother. By the grace of God, my wife and I were able to support each other emotionally and spiritually. On weeknights and weekends, I was either studying the Bible and the *Big Book* or helping minister to the house churches. This routine kept me sane through the end of my contract. My time in the desert allowed me to grow my relationship with God. It also strengthened my commitment to sobriety and spiritual growth.

When my two-year contract was complete, I took the opportunity to visit Jerusalem on my way home. I became a secret messenger for the house churches of Riyadh, carrying a large monetary donation to the Church of Bethlehem and some clothing for a Palestinian family in Old Jerusalem. The route went something like this: fly from Riyadh to Larnaca, Cyprus; take a cab to Limassol, Cyprus; catch the ferry from Limassol to Haifa, Israel; and take a bus from Haifa to Jerusalem. Reflecting on that journey, I had no idea what I was doing or how I was going to get to Jerusalem. God was guiding me. Leaving Saudi Arabia, no one can get a direct flight from anywhere in Saudi Arabia to

Israel. To the Saudi people, Israel does not exist. The trip took me twenty-four hours. I stayed in Jerusalem at the Hotel David for seven days, touring all the religious sights by myself.

I needed to contact the pastor of the Church of Bethlehem to give him the love offering from the Christians in Riyadh. I felt like James Bond when I left the hotel to use a payphone so that I could call the pastor of the Church of Bethlehem and set up a meeting. The pastor wanted to meet me at my hotel, but I thought that was somewhat conspicuous, but he said not to worry—that it would not be a big deal. We met in the hotel coffee shop, and I brazenly handed over $10,000 in a white envelope. I just knew that I was going to be arrested: I was scared to death that something terrible would happen, but it didn't.

The next challenge was delivering the clothes to the Palestinian family in Old Jerusalem after curfew. It took me forever to find the house. There aren't many street signs in Old Jerusalem, and at night the narrow streets are poorly lit. When I knocked, and the person who answered the door wasn't sure who I was. I told them that I was from Riyadh and that I knew their son, and these were gifts from him. They took them and closed the door. I stood there for a moment, then turned around and went back to the hotel. I thought that went as good as it could. Keeping everything anonymous was best, so I didn't give it another thought.

Two days later, I got a call from the grandfather of my Palestinian friend. He said that because of my generosity, he would give me a personal guided tour of all the Christian, Jewish, and Muslim religious sites in Jerusalem. He was a retired tour guide. I was truly blessed to have that special time with him. Because of that tour, I was able to go back to some special Christian sites and spend as much uninterrupted time alone as I wanted. The next day, I went to Old Jerusalem early in the morning to start my walk through history. During the mornings, all the street vendors had their booths open to selling trinkets and memorabilia to the hordes of tourists. On the Via Dolorosa (the fourteen stations of the cross), you could find just about every Christian symbol or artifact you would want. At first, I was bothered by the commercialism of the religious sites, but then I came to understand that this was the only way Palestinians who were living and working in Old Jerusalem could survive.

I continued my journey along the path that Christ walked, and soon it was high noon. A siren started to blare. Because of the Intifada, the Israeli military enforced a curfew for Old Jerusalem that meant that all the shops had to close. All the Palestinians in the area took their wares and left. The Israeli military began patrolling the streets of Old Jerusalem. I kept walking the streets of Old Jerusalem, sightseeing while the soldiers patrolled. I encountered a pair of Israeli soldiers who saw me but kept walking in a different direction. I took that as a sign that it was okay for me to stay in Old Jerusalem during the curfew, and I took advantage of the quiet solitude of the empty streets.

My first stop was to the Church of Golgotha, where Jesus hung on the cross. I spent an hour there in meditation. I was able to touch the large crack in the rock that split the moment Christ Jesus died. That experience shook my spiritual foundation and opened my eyes to the magnificent gift that God had given me as Christ paid for my sin. The next stop was to enter the Church of the Holy Sepulcher, the tomb of Christ. I was able to spend two hours alone in the tomb, praying and meditating on God's grace. I was able to spend the whole afternoon in deep spiritual fellowship with God. I will never forget this spiritual blessing. It consecrated my faith. To this day, I feel spiritually connected to my God as I reflect on how I was able to spend so much time in personal, intimate meditation with Christ Jesus and constantly relive those powerful experiences. The next two days, I visited Bethlehem, the Dead Sea, the Jordan River, Masada, The Garden Tomb, and Gethsemane. I was overwhelmed with the presence of God in my life.

My two years in Saudi Arabia and my week in Jerusalem allowed me to grow closer to God while in the desert, but now it was time to head home to the United States. When I arrived at the airport in Jerusalem, Israeli Security immediately took me to an interrogation room for questioning. I was afraid because I knew how skilled the Israeli Security was, and I wasn't sure if they would believe my account of my time in the Middle East. The Israeli military intelligence officers could not figure out how I got to Israel from Saudi Arabia and what my purpose was in coming to Israel. They were suspicious because I had spent two years in Saudi Arabia. They wanted to know why I went to Saudi Arabia and what I did while I was there. They asked me about my time in Jerusalem and finally released me. The Israeli Security had already processed my luggage, so I had to run to the departure gate to board the plane. I was the last person to board, and the pilot immediately began takeoff procedures. I caught the plane with only minutes to spare. America, here I come! I was so grateful to be on my way home. I have had an experience of a lifetime, but now it was time to get back to my wife and life in America.

CHAPTER 15

A NEW CAREER

After two years in Saudi Arabia and a visit to Israel, I started to get back into a routine with my family. Shirley and I were still living in Radcliff, Kentucky. My mother-in-law was in remission from cancer, and we were able to be a support to my wife's parents. My wife was working at the Army hospital as a nurse in the allergy clinic. Once again, I sent out resumes and went on a couple of job interviews, and still, I was overqualified. That's when I decided that it was time to go back to school.

I knew from my military experience and my time in the Saudi desert that my heartfelt passion was working with people. In the military, you were only as successful as how well you took care of your soldiers. In my recovery in AA, I have only been able to stay sober when helping another alcoholic or addict. The most dangerous place for me to spend any time is in my head. I can create all sorts of chaos and conjure up negative thoughts and feelings, leading to relapse. The best defense against that happening is reaching out and helping another alcoholic. This mentoring gets me out of my head and my negative feelings. It allows me to share my experience, strength, and hope and not focus on my issues. True immunity from drinking is only possible by working with other alcoholics. In my spiritual journey, peace and serenity came through service and fellowship with fellow believers. My dilemma was how to be of service and meet my spiritual needs. It became clear to me that the best opportunity I would have to meet my needs was to become a social worker. Because of my love for theology and the study of the Bible, I went to the Carver School of Social Work at the Southern Baptist Seminary in Louisville. I met with the dean for about an hour, and at the end of that time, it was clear to me that I was not a good candidate for their program.

I decided to go to the University of Louisville to talk with the administration at the Kent School of Social Work. I wanted to become a clinical therapist, doing psychotherapy with adults and practicing from a Christian perspective in Radcliff and Elizabethtown. I learned that I could do that, but it would take sixty credit hours to graduate from their clinical track. I also found out that I could go full time in their clinical path and complete the sixty hours in eighteen months instead of twenty-four months. I enrolled in Kent School in August 1990 and graduated in 1991 with a master of science in social work. I loved every one of my classes, even though I was a non-traditional student. Not only was I forty-eight years old, but I was a member of the defense establishment and a conservative Republican. I had fun challenging the younger students, as our worldviews seemed at odds.

Writing papers seemed to come naturally, even though I must confess that I would write all my papers by hand, and Shirley would type them up for me. She would frequently tell me that she didn't understand anything that I was writing. I would smile but be eternally grateful. I did both of my practicums at Fort Knox. The first practicum was with the behavioral health department of the Army hospital, where I worked with domestic violence offenders. That was an emotional challenge. It was an awkward time for me, because I was the only male social worker in the Behavioral Health Department of the hospital. My practicum happened during Operation Desert Shield, as soldiers deployed to Saudi Arabia to prepare for war with Iraq. The Fort Knox chaplains held a weeklong seminar for wives to help them deal with running the household by themselves. The seminar was held in the chapel with daycare provided. The problem was that the chaplains hadn't planned any activities for the children. The chaplains asked social workers from the hospital to come and work with the kids. I was part of that team. The children clung to me as I dragged them around the room, but the week drained me emotionally. I was happy that other social workers could work with kids, because I knew that I could not.

The second practicum was with the Community Counseling Center, where I had undergone the intensive outpatient program for my alcoholism. My counselor in 1983 was now the director of the clinic. We had a great relationship, and I fit right in with the staff there. I immediately had a caseload of clients. I had a great experience working with the military drug and alcohol treatment program and gained valuable experience dealing with the alcoholics and addicts and their commanders. From that practicum experience, I began to feel like I found my vocation—helping alcoholics and addicts. I was thriving in my fellowship, sharing my experience, strength, and hope to help other alcoholics. I was having so much fun in school. I enjoyed the entire experience.

I was about to graduate in December 1991 when I learned about a peer-driven social model that the Jefferson County Jail in Louisville was starting. I had tuition to pay back, so I was looking for a job in the treatment field. I contacted the program director of that peer-driven program and expressed my interest in working in the program. We met three times over the next two weeks, and each time that I walked away, I felt that we had a great relationship and that we could work together in this social model of treatment. We were about ready to close the deal when the director said that I would have to be interviewed by his staff—something he didn't think would be a problem for me. The staff interview was the following week held in the large front room of the jail. I arrived early and entered the room with a large banquet table with three chairs on one side and one chair on the opposite side. Naturally, I sat in the single chair and waited. Precisely at 9 a.m., three women walked (or marched) in and sat across from me. During the next ten minutes, I was asked question after question about my recovery, my twelve-step experience, and my counseling experience.

All the questions were utterly appropriate, but I panicked and choked. I could not even answer simple questions about my recovery or my experience working with alcoholics. The leader took sympathy on me and thanked me for coming for the interview, but it was evident that I was not experienced enough to work with them in the new venture. All three staff members wished me luck. I left sad. I didn't know where to turn to find a job in the addiction treatment field. I felt hopeless. What if I'm not able to work in this field? It had become my dream job, but I didn't have the appropriate experience or treatment knowledge and skills.

One day, Shirley was talking to her boss about my dilemma, and the clinic director said, "Get me his resume, and I'll see what I can do." I was so grateful. A couple of weeks later, I got a call asking me to come and interview for a position as executive director of the Jefferson County Medical Society (JCMS) Outreach Program. I didn't know what the organization was or what it did, but I agreed to go to the interview. The JCMS Outreach Program, Inc., began on August 15, 1989, operating a homeless shelter for men previously operated by Father John Morgan, which was called Mission House. I had the honor of meeting with Dr. Will Ward Jr., chairman of the board of JCMS Outreach Program, and Dr. Kenneth Peters, acting President of the Jefferson County Medical Society. These two visionary doctors, along with ten other doctors and five community leaders, had the vision and passion for forming the 501(c)(3) nonprofit board of directors to oversee and operate what came to be called the Morgan Center. The board of directors immediately began to operate the shelter. That interview turned out to be fifteen one-on-one meetings with individual board members of the JCMS Outreach Program.

I got the job. The board members believed that, with my military experience, I could run a homeless shelter. With any luck, I thought that I might be able to use my degree in social work to help the homeless men who used the shelter daily. I had no experience working with the homeless, and the only welfare experience that I had was helping the enlisted soldiers apply for food stamps. I had my own experience in recovery and had just celebrated eight years of sobriety. I was grateful for the opportunity but apprehensive about tackling a job so unfamiliar to me. How could a social worker with a military background and eight years of sobriety learn all about social welfare and the needs of the homeless? I planned to be a psychotherapist, and I thought, what opportunities would I ever have working with the homeless? God had a surprise waiting for me.

*The JCMS Outreach Program at the Morgan Center, 1020 West
Market Street, Louisville, Kentucky, in 1992.*

CHAPTER 16

A NEW SPIRITUAL
JOURNEY

It was December 15, 1991, when I walked through the front door of 1020 West Market Street in Louisville, Kentucky. For me, it was a new experience and a challenge of starting a new career in the field of social work. I began working for the JCMS Outreach Program operating the Morgan Center, a shelter that welcomed homeless men who may be under the influence of drugs and or alcohol. I met the staff for the first time. The shelter had a resident manager who had been in that role for eighteen years. He was responsible for the day-to-day activities of the shelter, which included checking in and out the homeless men who would stay overnight. The manager also supervised the three cooks and worked with the social worker who did case management for the men who needed help transitioning back into the community. The social worker successfully helped thirty men move from the shelter into independent living.

For the first month, I struggled with how a social worker (me) would manage the shelter. A retired military officer who was volunteering at St. John's Day Center, another homeless shelter in Louisville, invited me to lunch to talk about the Morgan Center. During lunch, my fellow officer asked how it was going at the Morgan Center, and I said I was struggling to try to figure out how to manage the shelter. He asked me, "What would you do in the Army when you took command of a new unit?" I responded that I routinely observed every aspect of the operations of the command for at least thirty days, if not longer, then made the changes that I thought would enhance performance. He told me that the shelter is no different than taking command of a new unit—do what I did in the Army. It was the best advice that I could have ever gotten. It took the pressure off me to try to be a social worker without any experience. I came to realize that people are the same everywhere. All they want is to be appreciated and supported, and, if you take care of them, they will take care of you.

God has a sense of humor because it wasn't long after that lunch when I had a visit from the director of the Coalition for the Homeless, the director of community affairs for the city of Louisville, and the director of social services for Jefferson County. During this "intervention," they told me that they were knowledgeable about all the many misdeeds that the resident manager had committed against the homeless men using the shelter over the last eighteen years. I said that I would not act on hearsay, so they said they would have some former shelter residents come and share their stories. A week later, the chairman of the JCMS Outreach Program board of directors and I met with two men who shared the stories of abuse that they suffered at the hands of the shelter's resident manager. After the meeting, the board chairman asked me what I was going to do about this situation. I replied that I was going back to the shelter and immediately fired the resident manager. The chairman agreed.

A week after I fired the resident manager, the social worker quit. For the next two weeks, I lived at the shelter, doing all of the check-ins, check-outs, and monitoring the culture of the men. I ran errands for the cooks and got supplies for each meal. Being with the clients every day, I got to know all of them. I had the opportunity to sit and listen to them and was able to call them by their first name. I was beginning to gain a little insight into life on the street. The Morgan Center was the only shelter in Louisville where men under the influence of drugs or alcohol could come and spend the night; it was their safe haven. I recognized that the men treasured the opportunity to spend the night in a safe place.

My first learning opportunity came when I decided to make the shelter a safe place. To make that happen, I didn't want any drugs, alcohol, or weapons in the sleeping area at any time. I procured small lockers, like the ones you'd find at a bus station, and had all the men lock their bags in those lockers before they went to the sleeping bay. I felt confident that now the shelter was safe. I thought I was smart by ensuring that there would be no weapons, alcohol, or drugs in the shelter. I did not anticipate how important it was for every man's personal peace of mind not to be separated from his weapon or the drugs or alcohol that was in their bag. Trying to enforce a rule that is impossible to enforce had everyone laughing at the rule.

After realizing how ineffective my approach was, I decided to get rid of the lockers and told all the men. I started a new policy: What's in the bag stays in the bag while they're at the Morgan Center. I said to them that this was their safe place, and it was up to them to make it safe. This policy created a culture of support and accountability among the men to make the shelter safe. The men appreciated our concern for their safety, and, because they valued the safe shelter, they wanted to keep the shelter safe. At this point, it was essential to establish some basic rules of conduct to support the shelter's safe place. There was zero tolerance on campus for using alcohol or drugs, any violence or threats of violence, any forms of racism, any forms of sexism, or stealing. Any violation of these rules meant automatic and immediate discharge from the shelter.

The policy of "what's in the bag stays in the bag" worked exceptionally well. On rare occasions, the staff found an empty whiskey bottle or pipe in the shelter. When that happened, we called everyone together and said, "Look, someone is violating the guidelines. You know who it is. Tell them to stop. None of us want to create a 'police state' here. Hold each other accountable." Because of that peer accountability, there have been very few incidents over the last thirty years. That culture of mutual accountability exists to this day and is the foundation of the social model recovery program.

Getting to know the men on a personal level made me realize that many of these men were addicted to drugs and/or alcohol. From my own recovery experience, I knew that, if any of these men were to realize their full potential, they needed to be clean and sober. I knew that the first step was to attract men to a place where they could begin the recovery journey. There had been a program called the Sobering Up Station that was run by another organization, but it had recently closed after the three-year demonstration grant ended. The Sobering Up Station was a twenty-bed facility where men under the influence could come and detox. During their stay in detox, the men were encouraged to connect with community resources to continue their recovery program. Over the three years, the program was very successful in reaching out to the men on the street and filling all twenty beds every day. It was more challenging to get the men to connect with community resources.

My vision was to replicate the Sobering Up Station. The previous executive director of the Jefferson County Medical Society Outreach Program had started a project to renovate the two buildings across the street from the Morgan Center, located at 1017 and 1019 West Market. There was a grant from the City of Louisville for $100,000 for renovation, and the plan was to do the work in phases as money became available. With my military experience, I knew that the phased plan had a high probability of not happening. I went to Jefferson County officials and secured another $100,000 grant and then asked the chairman of the JCMS Outreach Program board to raise another $100,000. With $300,000, I convinced the contractor, Jesse Bollinger, a JCMS Outreach Program board member, to renovate the two buildings for that amount, even though I knew it would take considerably more money. Jesse agreed to do the work. The renovation included an addition to 1019 West Market that would eventually become a Sobering Up Center, modeled after the Sobering Up Station that had closed. The renovation project began in January 1992.

Shortly into the renovation phase, I realized that I needed help running the day-to-day operations of the wet shelter. Monitoring the renovation and keeping up with all the required paperwork was consuming all my time. I hired a classmate from Kent School of Social Work to run the shelter while I oversaw the renovations. This person hired additional staff and began taking care of checking in and out the clients and supervising the cooks. Besides the overnight shelter, the Morgan Center offered soup and sandwiches during lunch for anyone in the community. The staff continued to run the wet overnight shelter while I managed the renovation of 1017 and 1019 West Market.

On September 21, 1992, the new Sobering Up Center officially opened. The staff and I were there to work and greet the men who were wanting to get clean. On the first day, no one came. On the second day, no one came. I was starting to get frustrated. I couldn't figure out why the men would not come in off the street to sober up. In hindsight, maybe they remembered their experience in the Sobering Up Station and didn't want to have the same experience. I was at a point to try anything to get someone to stay in the Sobering Up Center. I knew a homeless man was living in an abandoned truck parked next to the facility, so I sent the staff over to invite this man to come to the center to get a shower, a hot meal, and clean clothes. When he found out we wanted him to take a shower, he said no way and left. I was disappointed. It took a week to gain the trust of the street before men would voluntarily come to the Sobering Up Center to recover. What I learned from this experience is that the homeless alcoholics and drug addicts had gone to agencies or programs to receive help, but for various reasons, the support didn't happen. The men on the street were waiting to see if the Sobering Up Center staff would do what they said they would do. I learned the importance of "Say what you are going to do, and do what you say!"

Now that the Sobering Up Center was up and running, it was time to consider starting a recovery program for homeless men who were addicted to drugs and alcohol. With the board's approval, I began to set in motion the early steps of a recovery program. I had no idea how to build a recovery program but knew from my clinical studies at Kent School and my own twelve-step program that we needed to start with an alcohol-free shelter. Having men under the influence mingling with men trying to learn how to stay clean was an open invitation for relapse and drama. On the first Monday of October 1992, I decided that it was time to start the recovery program. I did the 3:30 p.m. check-in and did a sniff test. If the homeless man smelled of alcohol, I told him that he would not be allowed to come to the Morgan Center tomorrow. I checked in eighty men that night. Tuesday at 3:30 p.m., when I began admitting the men, there were only fifty. I asked where the other thirty were and learned they were trying to get into other shelters since they were under the influence.

Homeless men and women are very compliant; tell them what the rules are, and they will abide by them. That night, I got complaint calls from the staff of the other four shelters asking what was going on at the Morgan Center since clients were being kicked out. I told each one of them that we were developing a recovery program, starting with an alcohol-free shelter.

At 9 a.m. the next day, I looked out to Market Street, and men were marching up and down the street carrying placards saying, "Doctor's Rules Unfair! Shutting Out the Homeless!" There were homeless men in the middle of Market Street, handing out handbills with the same message. By 10 a.m., all four local television news stations and both newspapers had reporters and cameras in front of the Morgan Center wanting to know why the doctors were shutting out the homeless. How could the doctors be so heartless? My only reply was that the Morgan Center, operated by the Jefferson County Medical Society Outreach Program, was going to be a recovery program for alcoholics and addicts. The news story of the Morgan Center turning away homeless men was on all the television newscasts that night and in both of the main newspapers the next day.

Doctors were concerned about the publicity, because their calling is to heal and serve their patients and clients. Their creed is to "do no harm" and heal. The chairman of the board called an emergency meeting of the nine-member executive committee to decide how to respond to the publicity. The eighteen concerned board members met for two hours to discuss the option of a wet versus dry shelter.

The board chair finally took a vote with nine board members voting wet and nine voting dry. I was in a real pickle! How do I resolve this dilemma? I had to think fast. Realizing that 1020 West Market was a two-story building with sleeping areas on both floors, I quickly said, "Maybe we could do both, wet and dry. The second-floor sleeping area could be wet for the overnight guests, and the downstairs sleeping area could be the beginning of the recovery program." The board members asked how that could happen, and I said that I would need to hire more staff, which would increase the program cost by $100,000. The doctors said that they would raise the additional money, and they did just that.

This monumental decision became the core philosophy and the beginning of the social model recovery program that is still in existence today. I was lucky to have been able to dodge that bullet. Out of a mistake or error in judgment came the solution for thousands of men and women to achieve sobriety. I still had no idea how to go about building a recovery program. I knew it had to be a program of attraction, and based on the twelve steps. I also knew that I needed help.

The Healing Place—1017 and 1019 West Market Street in 1996.

The Healing Place—1020 West Market Street in 1996.

CHAPTER 17

REACHING OUT FOR HELP

The first ten months at the Morgan Center were stressful. Between running the shelter with the help of my classmate and supervising the renovation of 1017 and 1019 West Market, I was mentally and physically exhausted. I decided to take a short, five-day vacation. I left my classmate and staff in charge of running the day-to-day shelter operation. When I got back from vacation, I walked into my office to find the board chairman waiting for me. I asked why he was there, and he said that my classmate had requested an emergency meeting of the executive committee to present evidence about my incompetency in running the shelter. My classmate presented his case by saying that I had not started a recovery program yet, that I couldn't run it, and that I would never make any decisions. He told the board that I was not doing anything that they had directed. He concluded by saying the board that the reason that I was so incompetent was because I was an alcoholic.

The board chairman said that the committee responded by saying that I was accomplishing everything they had directed. Even though they did not know that I was a recovering alcoholic, my hire was even more appropriate. The chairman asked what I was going to do about my classmate. I replied that I was going to immediately go out front and fire my classmate and his support staff. I was starting all over again, running the shelter by myself. Some lessons are difficult and painful. What I learned later was that my classmate wanted to be the executive director and was doing everything possible to see me lose my job. I lost someone whom I believed to be a trusted friend.

Shortly after getting the job at the Morgan Center, I engaged a clinical supervisor to begin my clinical supervision for licensure as a licensed clinical social worker. When I told my clinical supervisor about my dilemma, he suggested that I contact a fellow drug and alcohol professional with twenty-five years of experience who was living in Shreveport, Louisiana, at the time. I called Chris Fajardo and asked if he would be willing to come to Louisville and consult with me for a couple of months and help build a recovery program. I gave Chris a brief description of what I had already had in place, told him about the social detox unit detoxing without medications for withdrawal symptoms, the wet overnight shelter on the second floor, and the abstinence-based recovery program on the first floor. I didn't have a curriculum but knew that the twelve-step principles for recovery had to be the basis. Chris was clear in stating that he didn't think mixing drinking with non-drinking would work but was willing to look at the possibilities.

Chris arrived the day after Thanksgiving 1992. Together, we began talking about twelve-step recovery and a program of attraction and accountability. During all the long hours we were together every day, we faced constant interruptions because of operational problems, and we struggled to put a model together. We plastered the walls with flip chart paper diagraming in concept the social model recovery program. We looked at the design from every angle, trying to identify unintended consequences. A couple of weeks later, we heard about a training conference that would provide lessons on how to teach the principles of a twelve-step recovery program. This course was to show the trainer how to implement a program called *Recovery Dynamics*. Chris and I were blown away by the depth and structure of the classes. This program of *Recovery Dynamics* would become the core curriculum for this new social model recovery program. By this time, Chris and I had built a rapport of creative inspiration, and I offered him the job of program director. He accepted, and together we began to create the pieces of a peer-driven social model recovery program.

CHAPTER 18

BUILDING A SPIRIT-FILLED RECOVERY PROGRAM

Over the last two weeks of December 1992, Chris and I were able to begin brainstorming ideas about how to build this program of attraction and accountability. We recognized that we needed to recruit alcoholics and addicts who had completed a recovery program. These men would become role models for men on the street, because they would have credibility. The program that I interviewed for back in 1991 had just completed its first year of using a social model of recovery. I contacted the executive director and asked if there were any alumni from the program who would be willing to come and work at the JCMS Outreach Program to help start a social model recovery program. The director said that there were four alumni, whom they called elders, who were interested in helping us build a program. They came in January 1993, and we started to make progress.

We had three paid cooks who worked one day on and two days off, feeding the overnight shelter guests and detox clients. We had the *Recovery Dynamics* curriculum, and we had staff to run the wet overnight shelter and the detox. We had four elders, whom we called assistant staff, begin building the recovery model. We hoped to attract men from the social detox and the overnight shelter to participate in our recovery program. We started to add services that included a daily free lunch in the soup kitchen, a clothing closet for the overnight guests, and a free medical clinic that was operated by volunteer doctors.

The basic principles of the social model recovery program were that everyone was entitled to be treated with dignity and respect, whether they were guests in our overnight shelter or the recovery program. That meant everyone should be called by their first name; everyone should experience unconditional love without expectation; everyone was expected to hold each other accountable for appropriate behavior and help to make change happen. Appropriate behavior, as defined by the twelve essential values of the twelve-step program, are:

> *These are the behaviors that everyone on the recovery journey strives to practice in their daily life. The more senior members of the community role model these behaviors and, in a loving way, hold their younger brothers and sisters accountable to learn these healthy behaviors.*

The detox and overnight shelter services are there to benefit anyone as an entitlement. *Entitlement* is a social welfare term, defining services and benefits provided to all citizens without cost to the individual. Providing the detox and overnight shelter services as an entitlement eliminates barriers and grants access to the recovery program. The social model recovery program is an empowerment, or self-determination, strength-based model that allows the individual to develop skills to become self-sufficient and independent. The foundation of this unconditional love is God's grace, allowing brothers and sisters to love each other to life, recognizing that they are their brother/sister's keeper. Every attempt by the staff is to meet the people where they are and raise the bar of expectation. The focus of the model is to reinforce daily that this disease of addiction is fatal and that the focus on recovery is daily. The focus is on the unity of purpose. The idea is to keep the program simple. Everyone in the recovery program is there for only one reason, to learn how to stay sober and have a meaningful, productive life. The focus is on recovery and nothing else. By eliminating as many outside distractions as possible, the men and women focus on themselves and learn how to make necessary behavioral changes. Everyone—staff and clients—reinforce the idea that all need to help each other recover. The design of the model is to reduce or eliminate all outside distractions to allow the alcoholic and addict time to make changes in their thinking and acting. The assistant staff would role model social skills for positive change while teaching and guiding the clients in the recovery program through the twelve-step program. The assistant staff would share their experience, strength, and hope.

Alcoholics and addicts avoid accountability. For change to occur, the alcoholic and addict must be confronted lovingly with rigorous honesty. The concept of a modified therapeutic, peer-driven community meeting helps to provide a forum for men in the recovery program to hold each other accountable for inappropriate behaviors. Recovery is assuming responsibility for self and others, and this means that the model is self-governing. Alcoholism and addiction are, at their core, a disease that fosters dishonesty, self-centeredness, and self-seeking, as well as many other forms of inappropriate, destructive behavior.

The community meeting is all about change. Self-destructive, inappropriate behavior that gets the addict into trouble with the law, their family, friends, or employers needs to change if the addict is to recover. Everyone in the recovery program is either a part of the problem or part of the solution. This community meeting occurs three days a week for one hour. During this meeting, peers address an individual's shortcomings or character defects and give suggestions showing how the individual could change his behavior.

I facilitated the community meeting only to keep the meeting focused on helping the individual being addressed and that only his peers would make suggestions on how the individual could change his behavior. Recommendations were written on the whiteboard, and the suggestion that received the most votes was offered to the individual. We refer to these suggestions as consequences or learning opportunities, not punishments. All alcoholics and addicts in the madness want to change; they just don't know what to change or how to change it. Suggestions for change from their alcoholic and addict peers are credible and effective.

The recovery program had now begun. The program started with ten men willing to start their recovery journey. The recovery program, with all its services, is provided at no cost to the client. As part of the social model, clients perform a series of tasks that keep the facility functioning, such as housekeeping and laundry. At first, I wanted to keep the paid cooks, because I was afraid that if men in the program were responsible for the meal, that they might leave the program and relapse without warning, and then there would be no food prepared for the overnight guests and the men in the program. I did think that it was a good idea to have the clients in the recovery program be responsible for the daily cleaning and laundry chores. My social work heart felt guilty about asking the men to do chores, so I implemented a plan to pay each client $5 for the first week of completing chores, $10 the second week, and $15 the third week. As an incentive, I also paid each of the men $1 for every lesson that they completed in *Recovery Dynamics*. After three weeks in the program, a man would get $15 a week plus $1 for every completed lesson, which could be an additional $28 by the end of all the classes.

After a couple of months, Chris told me that he thought the men would do the chores and complete the lessons without receiving any money. I said that I wasn't sure, but was willing to give it a try. I announced that six months from this date, we would no longer pay for the chores or the lessons. When the six-month deadline arrived, no one got paid, and there was not one complaint. I couldn't believe it. The men were so grateful for the program that they were willing to do anything and everything asked of them just to have the opportunity to learn the tools of recovery. The program continued to rock on and grow every day.

At one point, I became concerned about the number of men who had dropped out of the program within a couple of weeks of starting. There had to be some way of motivating them to want to stay and finish the program. I struggled with thinking about motivation and realized that the only way that I could see motivation is through action. I thought back to my first two weeks running the overnight shelter and remembered that two perks would affect change in a homeless person: a guaranteed bed every night and a place to store their belongings. The guaranteed bed every night provided the security needed for the individual who no longer needed to worry about where he was going to sleep. The opportunity to store all of his belongings during the day meant that, while he was out on the street during the day, he would not look homeless. He would have dignity and be respected as a human being. During the day, the overnight shelter beds were empty, since check-in happened at 3:30 p.m. each day. For a man who wanted to start his recovery journey, we would guarantee bed number "Six Up" for a week and let him store his belongings under that bed. To keep that bed for the next week, instead of wandering the streets, he has to attend two recovery classes off campus every day.

This part of the model became known as the motivational track. The location we originally called the Freedom Center was about two miles away from the main campus. The men were required to trudge (walk with a purpose) to and from the Freedom Center every day virtually without regard to bad weather. They trudged to get their alcohol or drugs, so they needed to trudge to get their recovery. This trudging became a critical part of the model, along with the community meeting, held three days a week. Not only was this trudging healthy for the men to walk four miles a day, but the trudging also allowed them to start building trusting relationships with their peers. They would make behavioral contracts with each other and hold each other accountable when they began to think about leaving the program or going to see their drug dealer or doing inappropriate behavior. The men realized that their behavior twenty-four hours a day, seven days a week, affected how the public perceived the quality and effectiveness of the social model recovery program and the Morgan Center.

At the Freedom Center, there were classes at 10 a.m. and 1 p.m. Free lunches were available at various shelters around the city. The men would come back to the main campus by 2:30 p.m. to attend a class at 3 p.m. with men who were in the recovery program. They obtained signatures for every class they attended and every AA meeting they attended. Each week, those sign-in sheets would be given to the assistant staff. The man with the most classes and AA meetings attended would move to a bed that was physically closer to those in the recovery program. Movement through the motivational phase is causally related to how many classes and meetings the person attended. Those who put forth the effort moved quickly through this phase. Those who were not moving as fast could only look at their level of commitment to attend more classes and meetings. It is peer role modeling.

The purpose of the social model is to require action to demonstrate motivation, then build a system of rewards to acknowledge that individual action. It's not enough to know that you are changing mentally; we all need rewards for completing tasks or requirements. On average, the men would be on the motivational track for up to ninety days before getting into the recovery program. By that time, they had generally attended sixty classes and more than 120 AA meetings. They had invested their only asset—time. The dropout rate was less than 30 percent. When a man finally got into the recovery program, he committed to complete the remaining classes during the next four months. The dropout rate in the recovery program was less than 5 percent. The social model recovery program is self-paced and based on the individual's effort to attend classes and complete the homework assignments.

The social model program is a treatment protocol defined as an established code of behavior or learning in an organization. In this protocol, everyone attends the same classes and completes the same homework throughout the twelve-step curriculum. It becomes individualized as each person accomplishes these tasks at their own, individual pace. The model is a long-term, intense, residential-recovery social model program located within an emergency shelter with a social detoxification unit. With a social detox, an overnight shelter, a motivational track, and a recovery program, the facility began to attract more and more men. Single beds became bunk beds, and more men were able to start their new life in recovery.

CHAPTER 19

SUPPORT AND ATTACK = THE MODEL SURVIVES

As the single beds became bunk beds, the recovery program started to grow. The detox unit remained full most of the time, the motivational track grew to a total of sixty men, the recovery program grew to fifty men, and the alumni phase grew to thirty men. The average length of stay for the whole program was about six months. All the men would complete the twelve-step program by attending twenty-eight classes and completing the corresponding lessons.

There were three significant events in 1995. First, the board of directors decided that the name Jefferson County Medical Society Outreach Program did not tell the story of what happened in the recovery program. What doctors do best is heal, so they debated for hours on appropriate names such as Healing Corner, Healing House, Healing Block, Healing Street, and Healing Place. Finally, they voted, and The Healing Place was selected. Years later, an alumnus came to me and said that the board did a great job in naming the program. I replied that yes, they did, because that's what the program does—heal. The alumnus said, "No, you don't get it. The Healing Place or THP. *THP* is The Higher Power!" What a name for the program. By accident, The Higher Power was in the name of the recovery program.

Late in 1994, The Healing Place was projecting a budget shortfall of $150,000 by the end of the next year. We sent letters requesting funding to Louisville's mayor and the Jefferson County Judge Executive. The mayor said that they get all their funding from the county and could not help. The county suggested that The Healing Place needed to do better financial planning and budgeting and that the county was not able to help. The board of directors decided that the only recourse was to close the twenty-four-bed social model detox to avoid the budget shortfall. Fortunately, the Kentucky Division of Substance Abuse in Frankfort realized how vital the detox was to the Louisville community as well as the state. The division was able to allocate the $150,000 to The Healing Place to cover the budget shortfall. Because The Healing Place was now receiving public funding for the detox operation, the detox had to be licensed as a non-medical detoxification unit by the state.

The Healing Place Center director for daily operations was a young woman who repeatedly asked me when we were going to start a recovery program for women. There was not a day that went by when she didn't ask me that question. Because of the state funding for the detox, there was also interest in wanting to see a women's program at The Healing Place. Libby Jones, wife of then-Kentucky Governor Brereton Jones, and her staff came to visit The Healing Place to ask what it would take to start a women's recovery program in Louisville. I replied, "Money." The First Lady asked how much, and I replied about $150,000. I told her that we could start the program as soon as we got the money, and Mrs. Jones said she could send the money as soon as she had a proposal. A week later, The Healing Place women's program began in a three-bedroom rental house located at 720 East Oak Street. The program quickly grew. There was a five-bed detox, one bed for an overnight guest, and ten beds for the recovery program.

The women's recovery program stayed full all the time, and the men's program continued to grow. There were fewer and fewer beds available for alumni who completed the program. For us to meet the need for sober living for the alumni, we leased two houses for the men completing the program. These houses provided thirty alumni with a place to live after they finished The Healing Place program.

In 1996, The Healing Place was approached by the leadership at the Hope Center in Lexington, Kentucky, that asked about the social model recovery program and if it was possible to replicate the model. After several visits to Lexington, the decision was made that The Healing Place model could and would be replicated. Three staff members from Louisville moved to Lexington and began building a social model recovery program there. The Hope Center rapidly began growing its recovery program, meeting a great need in the Fayette County area. It continues to help men and women today.

In 1997, a local contractor and developer came to The Healing Place board and said that he had a dream to build a large residential facility without a kitchen. He said that it didn't make any sense to him but wondered if The Healing Place would be interested. The Healing Place was interested because there was a considerable need for housing for alumni after they completed the recovery. If it was on campus, the current kitchen could provide the meals. The board approved the idea and applied for low-income housing tax credits, and the building at 1000 West Market Street became a reality. When construction finished, alumni moved out of the two rental houses and into the new facility at 1000 West Market. The houses were given to the women's recovery program, allowing it to grow from twenty-five to sixty. Both programs began to thrive.

Then 1997 happened. It became the year from hell. Attacks from every direction threatened to close The Healing Place recovery program because "it was doing treatment without a license." The challenges came from professionals in the drug and alcohol treatment field as well as former clients. During that year, every state agency inspected The Healing Place to determine if there were any violations or unethical practices. These were trying times for all the staff. Complaints of unethical treatment practices were filed against the licensed staff of The Healing Place. All the allegations in inspection reports and individual licensure complaints were answered in writing. After nine months of visits and inspections, the Director of the Kentucky Division of Substance Abuse asked the Secretary of Health and Human Services to issue a ruling that stated The Healing Place social model recovery program was a mutual-help, twelve-step, peer-driven program that did not need to be licensed by the state. The Secretary agreed and wrote a formal opinion stating that The Healing Place does not need to be licensed by the state as a treatment program. The Healing Place continued to grow every day.

In 1998, a nationwide survey from the Bureau of Primary Health Care asked clinics and healthcare providers to respond by indicating all the services provided and their willingness to be replicated. Representatives from the Bureau for Primary Health Care in Washington, DC, came to visit The Healing Place to verify all the services that we had reported in their survey of clinics. They could not believe all the services that The Healing Place was providing. After a four-day visit, the team left saying that we were providing even more services than we reported in the survey. Shortly after the group returned to Washington, they announced that The Healing Place was one of five programs being recognized nationally as "Models That Work" and should be replicated nationwide.

This recognition became the starting point for replication in other communities. The "Models That Work" designation interested community leaders and stakeholders from Raleigh, North Carolina, and they came to Louisville to visit The Healing Place. The group attended a community meeting then took a client-led tour of the program. The group went back to Raleigh on a mission; they wanted The Healing Place model in Raleigh. Our staff began to work with the newly established board of directors in Raleigh to begin replicating a one-hundred-bed facility for men with a detox unit. The Healing Place provided start-up staff to start operating the recovery program as well as additional assistance to establish the necessary infrastructure support. The project in Raleigh was a lot of fun for The Healing Place, as it was the first significant replication outside of Kentucky. A year and a half later, The Healing Place of Wake County opened, and it began to see the success of the social model—helping alcoholics and addicts recover and live a productive and meaningful life of sobriety. It was exciting to see the model shared to reach an underserved population. With the replication in North Carolina complete, the men's program in Louisville had grown to capacity.

The detox unit at 1017 and 1019 West Market, the recovery program at 1020 West Market, and the transitional housing at 1000 West Market were full all the time. There were more than 200 men on campus every day.

Meanwhile, the women's program was struggling to build and maintain a positive community recovery culture. Because the women were living in three separate houses, it was difficult for the women to bond and develop a sense of unity. During a board meeting, one of the members asked why there were only sixty women in the program. Having to think quickly, the only response that I had was that we needed a larger facility. The board committed to raising the money to expand the women's program. The Healing Place went to the Louisville Board of Aldermen and asked for funding to build a new facility for the women. One alderman pledged $150,000 to start the campaign to create a new women's campus. We also applied for a three-year, $300,000 matching grant from the Robert Wood Johnson Foundation—and we received it. Three local organizations, Gheens Foundation, Humana Foundation, and Norton Healthcare Foundation, pledged funding. So, the matching grant turned those $300,000 commitments into $600,000. The funding from the Robert Wood Johnson Foundation depended on us finding a location for the new women's campus and having a successful site visit by foundation staff. This process took a lot of time, so much so that the alderman's $150,000 pledge would come close to expiring within a couple of days.

Feeling a sense of urgency, a board member was driving down West Broadway when he spotted a for sale sign on a set of three buildings that formerly housed a motel. The board member called the realtor that night, asking if the buildings were still for sale. The answer was yes; the sale price $125,000. The board member said "Sold!" and then went to the full board the next day. He asked for forgiveness in making the decision but said that he knew that he had done the right thing. The facility had fifty-two rooms with fifty-two bathrooms, a kitchen, and a large dining room. What used to be a rent-by-the-hour motel would become a long-term, residential recovery center for women. Still, the plan was not without some opposition.

Soon after the sold sign went up on the building, The Healing Place received a cease and desist letter from an attorney who represented Jefferson County Public Schools. There was a public elementary school located behind the hotel, and the school was opposed to a men's recovery program being located so close. The school had appealed to the JCPS superintendent to stop The Healing Place from putting a recovery program next to it. At our request, several board members and I met with the deputy superintendent and his staff to explain how the recovery model worked. When we told them that this program was for women, not men, the deputy superintendent and his team became very supportive of the project. We walked away grateful that we had successfully dodged a bullet that would have killed the project.

Without resolution, we would have lost the grants from the city alderman and the Robert Wood Johnson Foundation.

We felt like we were home free. We were wrong. There was more opposition, this time from other drug and alcohol treatment providers. Some believed that The Healing Place staff had little or no experience working with women and women with children. They said we had no business telling the Robert Wood Johnson Foundation that we were competent to establish and run a recovery program for women, even though we had been operating that same program for four years. We were just forty-five days out from the Foundation's visit. I put together a proposed itinerary and sent it to the Foundation staff. I explained in detail that, in addition to all of the supporters and community stakeholders they would meet, they would also meet agency representatives who believed that The Healing Place had no business operating a women's program. The Foundation staff thought that idea was interesting and challenging.

The two staff members from the Robert Wood Johnson Foundation who visited were social workers who said that they were impressed with our planned support services and the substance abuse recovery program for the women's facility. The visit went exceptionally well. Halfway through their visit, we scheduled a meeting with supporters as well as those opposed to the project. During that meeting, our supporters talked long and loud about how good the women's current recovery program was and that, with the support of the Robert Wood Johnson Foundation, even more women would have access to recovery. The three agency representatives in opposition said a couple of sentences in disagreement, but their protests fell on deaf ears. After the meeting, we laughed when the Foundation staff said that they had not seen that much in-fighting since the 1970s. Our visitors from the Robert Wood Johnson Foundation returned to Pennsylvania, and we shortly received notification that we would receive the full $300,000 matching grant. Another victory for women's recovery!

1997 groundbreaking for the new building at 1000 West Market Street.

The Healing Place receives the "Models that Work"
recognition by BPHC, Washington, DC.

Dr. Will W. Ward was recognized for his service in 2002.

CHAPTER 20

REPLICATION, EXPANSION, AND DEATH

Soon after the women's recovery program opened at Sixteenth and Broadway, we had ninety-two clients enrolled. This was the first time that all the women were together on the same campus in the same building. The women's recovery program began to flourish. It was magical and spirit-guided.

The Healing Place continued to grow and provide recovery services to 250 men and one hundred women daily. In 2005, community leaders from Richmond, Virginia, became interested in our social model recovery program. The executive director of Caritas of Richmond contacted me to ask that The Healing Place come and replicate its model in Richmond. I sent our current men's program director to Richmond with accompanying staff to replicate the model. The program director did a great job in establishing our recovery program in Richmond, and, after six months, it was operating at full strength. Personal circumstances changed for our program director, and Caritas leadership asked him to stay and run the social model recovery program that he has just built. It was an offer of a lifetime for him, and I could only support his decision to stay in Richmond. It turned out to be the best decision for both programs. I was able to promote a talented staff member to become the new men's program director in Louisville.

Around this time, Don Ball, the chairman of the board at the Hope Center in Lexington, began working with the Kentucky governor, chairman of the Kentucky Housing Authority, and the director of the Kentucky Department of Corrections to put together an initiative called Recovery Kentucky. The idea was to fully fund the construction of a one-hundred-bed facility and fund the annual operating costs of The Healing Place's social model recovery program to be established in small rural communities throughout Kentucky.

The Kentucky Housing Authority would fund construction of each facility, and the Kentucky Department of Corrections would contract for fifty beds, paying a per diem for operating expenses for inmates to enter the recovery program at each one of these facilities. The Governor's Office for Local Development would provide a grant for the remaining balance of funding for the annual operating costs. The Healing Place began replicating its first model in Henderson, Kentucky, in the summer of 2007. Because of this initiative, The Healing Place's social model recovery program has now been replicated in fourteen rural communities across Kentucky, making recovery accessible without having to go to Louisville, Lexington, or northern Kentucky.

At one of the board meetings in 2006, I was asked why the women's program was so much smaller than the men's. At that time, the men's program was helping 225 men every day, compared to the ninety-two at the women's campus. I danced around the question until I thought of a plausible answer, and all I could come up with was the facility could only hold ninety women. The board decided that the women in our program deserved a facility that provides services for 200 women. The board committed to raising $20 million to build a new women's campus to help more women, and we launched a capital campaign to raise the philanthropic dollars to fund the construction of the new facility. As we created the financing strategy, it was time to find a suitable location for this new, 200-plus-bed facility. Funding would come from low-income tax credits for construction along with grants from the Gheens Foundation and the Kresge Foundation and raising pledges. A couple of board members and I went to West Louisville, looking for at least two acres of open land where we could build the new campus. We found several locations, including a sizable eight-acre, asphalt lot near a public housing development at Fifteenth and Hill Street. The surrounding area was light industrial with very few homes. I crossed that location off the list because it was in a dangerous part of town known for drug deals and prostitution. I thought that the other sites were much more suited for a women's recovery program, but I was feeling the pressure to find a suitable location for the new campus.

I had a staff member suggest that it might be a good idea to ask the women's program staff to look at all the proposed sites and tell me where they thought that the new campus should be. The women's program director called me around 6:30 p.m. on a Wednesday, trying to tell me what they had seen, but all I could hear were cheers, shouts, and clapping in the background. I asked the program director if they had found a location for the new women's campus, and she said yes—at Fifteenth and Hill. I said, "Oh, no! That is the worst location in the city with all the crime and prostitution. Why did you all pick that location?" She said, "We prayed about it. This is where the need is, and this is where we need to be!" There was nothing left for me to say except let's move forward and buy the property so that the architects can begin developing the plans for construction so that the women's program could have a new home.

We broke ground on the new facility at Fifteenth and Hill in the summer of 2008, and, eighteen months later, the women moved from Sixteenth and Broadway into the new 73,000-square-foot facility at Fifteenth and Hill. Two months after the new campus opened, the women's program had grown to 136 women. Today, that same facility provides services to 265 women every day. Wow! What a blessing it was to turn eight acres of asphalt into a green space of recovery for addicted women.

As we were finishing construction on the new women's campus and opening it in 2009, I had a significant catastrophe that blew up my personal life.

My wife, Shirley, had been diagnosed with multiple sclerosis when she was in her early thirties and lived relatively symptom-free for forty years. When she turned seventy, she started to have problems with her motor coordination and balance. On the advice of her internist, she began going to the gym daily to build up leg strength and strengthen her core. I thought that this was a great idea, so much so that I adjusted my work schedule at The Healing Place so that my wife and I could work out together. It was a lot of fun and an excellent opportunity to spend time together.

It was our usual practice to go to the neighborhood Mexican restaurant after our workout to have dinner. While we were at the restaurant in May 2009, my wife tried to order a bean burrito, but her words were so garbled that she gave up after three tries and started laughing. I wasn't laughing—I recognized the symptoms of a stroke. I broke out in a sweat. My heart pounded, and all I could think was, "Oh no, my wife is going to die." I told her that she needed to go to the hospital right now. To this day, I do not understand why I let my wife drive home with me following so that one car would be at home. Hindsight says that was absolutely the worst idea ever.

I got her to the hospital, and the staff immediately sent her for a CAT scan. Back in the emergency room cubicle, Shirley still could not speak clearly. It was about this time that our daughter arrived. I went out of the cubicle to talk to the doctor about the three-hour time limit stroke victims have for administering the anti-stroke injection. Two and a half hours had already elapsed, and I didn't know what to do. Should I permit the shot or not? My wife solved that problem when she had another seizure in the ER cubicle. After the second CAT scan, decisions became more difficult because both scans were negative. My wife was intubated and transferred to a room in the hospital's intensive care unit. My other daughter came up from Georgia, and the three of us kept watch over my wife. Throughout the night, her vital signs were normal. The three of us kept vigil all night. My oldest daughter told me to go home, get a shower, and rest. I left at 4 a.m. and returned to Shirley's bedside two hours later. Shortly after I returned, we were able to convince the staff that, because of her normal vital signs throughout the night, the breathing tube should come out. The tube came out, and Shirley's speech was almost perfect. I was relieved. A calm came over me, and I was able to start breathing again. I went downstairs to meet with the on-call neurologist to get the story on what had happened. The neurologist said that Shirley had had a significant stroke and that there was evidence of a history of several minor strokes. I asked him what we should do. We had a Panama Canal cruise booked in three weeks, and his advice was to keep on living, because we didn't know when the next stroke would come, so live life to the fullest. The neurologist said that my wife could have another stroke at any time, so make the most of the time you have left. That advice wasn't very comforting.

We went on the cruise, but I was worried the entire time. What if Shirley had another seizure while on the ship? How could I relax and enjoy the cruise? What will I do? The first night out of port, we joined an open table seating for dinner, and we were the last of four couples to be seated at our table. I must pause here for a moment and remind myself that God is always taking care of us, even when we can't take care of ourselves. Nothing in this world happens by accident. We had just sat down and begun to eat our appetizers when my wife casually mentioned to the woman sitting next to her that she had suffered a stroke weeks earlier. The woman replied, "Don't you worry. My husband is a neurologist. Here is our cabin number and cell phone number. You call us any time, day or night, while on the cruise and he will help." I nearly collapsed with relief, knowing that there was help available if we needed it. The rest of the ten-day cruise was indeed a blessing for my wife as it was her lifelong dream to cruise through the Panama Canal. I'll never forget this scene. Shirley is standing as far forward on the bow of the cruise ship, arms raised and in awe of passing through the Panama Canal. It was reminiscent of the scene from the movie *Titanic*.

Another blessing was that we had coordinated with the ship's staff to have the captain perform a renewal of our wedding vows. It was a special moment because we had made these arrangements before my wife had had her stroke. Little did we know the significance of that ceremony and how it fit into God's plan for our time together.

A week after we got home, Shirley went in for a follow-up MRI. She and I sat down with the neurologist and stared at the tumor in my wife's head. It had only been thirty days since her two normal CAT scans in the hospital emergency room, but now we were looking at a stage four tumor that was larger than a golf ball. It had grown during those thirty days and was inoperable. The only treatment was radiation and chemotherapy. I panicked. My heart broke. How was I going to deal with this? Because Shirley was a nurse, she knew this was a terminal condition, but I was in denial. I couldn't deal with the news. I didn't want to accept the diagnosis, and I didn't want to look at the MRI any longer.

Once again, God was looking out for us, and by us, I specifically mean me. I needed God more than ever. Shirley's diagnosis was to be the most difficult trial in my life. How could I deal with her dying? Because I was blessed to be working at The Healing Place, the staff covered for me and allowed me to be my wife's caregiver twenty-four seven. I was able to be with her pretty much all of the time, only taking breaks to come to Louisville for a few hours two or three times a week so that I could do some face-to-face work. I was able to spend the last nine months of our marriage together, loving my wife and taking care of her. She received radiation treatments three times a week for six weeks without complications. Following a short rest period, my wife's chemotherapy began. The chemo was administered once a week for every three weeks to stop and reduce the growth of the tumor. By October, it was clear that the chemo was not stopping the tumor's growth. I convinced my wife to endure two more chemo treatments to allow the family to celebrate Thanksgiving and Christmas. She agreed. We all spent our last holidays together as a complete family. Had it not been for the support and prayers of my brothers and sisters in AA, the wonderful staff of The Healing Place, and the board of directors, I would never have survived this heartbreak.

Shirley, my wife of thirty-six years, died on January 8, 2010, from a terminal brain tumor. I was devastated. My life mate and soulmate were gone. How could I go on? Life ceased to exist for me. There was nothing left for me to live for, and life had no meaning.

We had her memorial service in Elizabethtown with my eleven-year-old granddaughter delivering the eulogy. Another memorial service happened at The Healing Place women's campus. The love and support from everyone helped sustain and support my family and me through this horrible and unpredicted loss. Only by God's magnificent grace, the support of AA, and The Healing Place was I able to endure and move forward. Life goes on, so I went on living. I had the most wonderful job and staff to work with at The Healing Place. I had season tickets for University of Louisville football and basketball, and I had my houseboat on the lake for the summer. My life was structured and complete. But I was emotionally and mentally numb, trying to find myself once again. If it weren't for my church family, my sponsor, and the fellowship of my brothers and sisters in recovery, I would have been completely lost.

In 2011, the Kentucky Housing Corporation came to The Healing Place, asking if we would consider assuming ownership of the Recovery Kentucky facility in Campbellsville. Because the facility used our social model recovery program, it was merely a discussion of how the transfer of ownership would happen. The funding model for Recovery Kentucky provided the annual operating expenses. The Healing Place in Louisville assumed ownership and began operating the facility in Campbellsville, which continues to this day to serve one hundred men every day.

To help offset the cost to operate The Healing Place every year, I was always looking for additional revenue. Several years back, in 2012, the Department of Corrections had indicated that there was a need for more community-based substance abuse recovery programs. I knew the building at 1000 West Market named the Brady Center (after Dr. Burns Brady, who was the volunteer Medical Director for The Healing Place) currently housed our men who had completed the recovery program. This building would be an ideal facility for providing a substance abuse program for those coming out of prison and in need of treatment. Believing that the Department of Corrections would soon contract with The Healing Place for these beds, I naively began to make space in the building for the new program. About thirty alumni were living in the thirty-five rooms of the building. We started finding transitional housing for each one of the men. It took about two months to find responsible, ac- countable, supportive housing for all the men. September went by with no contract. October passed, and so did November. Finally, I could not wait any longer. The Healing Place was losing money every day that those rooms sat empty. Before this circum- stance, we at least had alumni paying a nominal rent each week. In desperation, I pleaded with the Department of Corrections to tell me what they could do in the way of a per diem contract for services. It turns out that the Department of Corrections needed help in finding transitional housing for male inmates who were serving out the last six months of their sentence. They would pay a per diem for each inmate housed in our building that would serve as transitional housing. The contract provided for up to 140 beds. The average daily census would be ninety to one hundred, which has remained constant.

Our new Women's Campus, located at Fifteenth and Hill, opened in 2009.

CHAPTER 21

THE HEALING PLACE IN SUCCESSFUL TRANSITION

It was now 2013, and the drumbeat coming from the board of directors of The Healing Place was getting louder and louder: "What is the succession plan, Jay?" "What happens if suddenly you are no longer with The Healing Place?" "Who is going to lead the organization?" I had already thought about these questions and had plans in place. In 2008, I had brought back a long-time friend of The Healing Place—Karyn Hascal—to serve as the vice president for mission advancement. Her responsibility was to look at everything The Healing Place did at all levels and ask why. I knew that this would help establish continuity and uniformity between programs, and this would provide an opportunity to refresh her understanding of The Healing Place's social model of recovery. After five years as vice president, she assumed the role of president of The Healing Place while I assumed the role of executive chairman. Succession planning was taking place.

In 2014, the opioid epidemic started to take hold in Louisville, Kentucky, and the rest of the country. It was becoming headline news, even though we had been seeing a growing number of individuals addicted to heroin and opiates in our detox unit for at least a year. More and more pressure was being put on treatment facilities to address the need and stem the tide of overdose deaths. We felt the pressure at The Healing Place. And we knew that we could easily expand our detox at the men's campus from twenty-four beds to fifty. We knew the need was real. We were starting to turn away from detox 200 to 300 men every month who wanted help—we just didn't have the beds. As we thought more about the magnitude of the problem, we realized that creating more detox beds was not the solution; that would only create a revolving door from detox to the street and back. What was needed was an expanded men's campus to provide both an increased number of detox beds as well as more recovery beds to help break the cycle of addiction.

We went to the board with the idea that The Healing Place's role in dealing with the opioid epidemic was to build an expanded campus for men that would include a larger detox and enough beds for the expanded recovery program. The men's current campus was a collection of buildings pulled together over the last twenty-nine years, and we really couldn't fit any more beds into the existing space. It was time to launch a new capital campaign to build a new men's campus to meet the demands for help. The Healing Place board and staff committed to raising $29 million to build a new 102,000-square-foot facility for 426 men. The staff and the board of directors rose to the challenge, making calls to donors and asking the Kentucky Housing Corporation for help in funding the foundation to build the new campus.

In January 2012, a miracle occurred in my personal life. I met a wonderful woman named Jackie who had become a new spark in my life. I say a new spark because, two years prior, my daughter had come to me and said, "Dad, you don't have any spark in your life." I told her that I did—I had my University of Louisville football and basketball season tickets and my houseboat in the summer. What more could a man ask? She disagreed and helped me put my information into a couple of dating websites. When we finished, I went to the lake for the Fourth of July holiday weekend. I returned home four days later and checked the sites and, to my surprise, I had many likes. I got scared and shut down the computer. I checked the sites a couple of days later and saw this fantastic woman who loved grandchildren and was a fanatic U of L fan, just like me.

Jackie and I started to date, pledging that we were not interested in marriage. We both had done that and were through with that type of commitment, but you know how that goes. We just wanted to be friends and have opportunities to have fun. We became best friends and realized that we did not want to be apart. On January 10, 2014, we got married on the beach in St. Croix with beachcombers as witnesses. I have been blessed ever since that day with a supportive, loving wife who believes in the mission of The Healing Place. She supports me and is my anchor. She has truly put the "spark" into my life. I am a whole person. Once again, God is doing for me what I can't do for myself. What a blessing.

It was January 2017 when construction of the new men's campus became a reality. The Healing Place broke ground, and the work got underway on phase one of the construction. We built the new facility in two phases, which would allow us to continue providing services to 250 men during construction. The phase one building contained the kitchen, dining room, a twenty-eight-bed detox, and enough beds to house all 250 men. There was even an elevator. Phase one construction finished on December 27, 2017, and clients moved into the new building. The first part of the new building meant that this was the first time in the history of the men's campus that the facility was totally handicap accessible. It was also just in time to lease up the beds in phase one to comply with the tax credit requirements. While phase one of the new building was happening, a new administration building was going up as well. Unbeknownst to me, the board of directors and executive staff officially dedicated this building as the Jay P. Davidson Administration Building. I was humbled and overcome with emotion. I couldn't keep a dry eye. Clients, staff, alumni, and board members were there to celebrate the dedication. I was overwhelmed with joy and gratitude.

In January 2018, construction crews demolished the existing building at 1020 West Market to make room for the phase two of construction, which would add twenty-two more beds for detox, a large classroom, a clinic, and multiple offices for the staff to provide services for 426 men daily. Phase two finished up just after Christmas that year. What a gift! The entire project finished on time, under budget, and with only $2 million left to raise. The Healing Place team and the board of directors accomplished a monumental task. They all are truly remarkable people who can achieve great things. It is a blessing to be able to work with such passionate and dedicated people.

The expanded men's campus located at Tenth and Market opened in 2018.

Now, what does the future hold for me and The Healing Place? I continue to trust God, clean house, and help another suffering alcoholic. The Healing Place is currently in the process of replicating our model in Wilmington, North Carolina. The replication will be 100 beds for women and one hundred beds for men. Both programs will be located on the same property, but each will retain its own, separate identity. There will be separate facilities for each program, and the schedule will allow each program to use the same classroom and dining room at different times. Both programs will have their own detox facilities. The newest replication is another new challenge for The Healing Place social model recovery program. It will work and be just as successful.

Will I ever retire from The Healing Place? I love this opportunity to share my experience, strength, and hope, so I doubt that I will ever retire. If there is a need, I will suit up and show up. Father John Morgan told me thirty years ago, "Don't rest on your laurels! It's not what you have done. It's what you have yet to do, because there are more people out there that need your help."

So, in memory of Father Morgan, I will get busy and do the next right thing.

WHY IT WORKS

The Healing Place has twenty-seven critical elements for fidelity for the Bio-Psycho-Social-Spiritual, long-term, residential, social model of recovery. It is essential to recognize that this is a recipe for success. Let's say that you like my chocolate cake so much that you ask me for the recipe. I give you a detailed list of ingredients and step-by-step procedures to make my chocolate cake. You're in your kitchen about to make my cake, but you decide to modify my recipe. You reduce the amount of sugar by half and add in more cocoa powder and chocolate chips. In the end, you will have a chocolate cake, but it won't resemble my chocolate cake because you have changed the recipe. Replicating The Healing Place social model of recovery requires that you adhere to the twenty-seven critical elements for fidelity.

Guiding and directing the client through the twelve steps of AA to find their own Higher Power is critical to the individual's ability to stay sober. The act of going systematically through the twelve-step process results in a psychic change referred to as a spiritual experience or a spiritual awakening.

Teaching the Sober 180 (**a twelve-step curriculum**) is the foundation for learning how to implement the steps and change behavior. Alcoholics and addicts don't know what behaviors need to change, and, even if they did know what had to change, they don't know how to change those behaviors. The *Sober 180* curriculum gives the alcoholic and addict insight into what and how to change.

Within The Healing Place, there are several levels of a **social community**. Each level of the model supports the recovery philosophy. The focus is on recovery starting in detox and overnight, continuing into the motivational track, and onto the completion of the steps, which culminate in continuing to practice these principles as an alumnus of the program.

The modified therapeutic, peer-driven community and the community meeting conducted three times a week are critical to a successful recovery program. Peers helping peers learn how to change is the cornerstone building block of the community process. The interaction of all the clients on a daily basis is the catalyst for change. The community meeting, held three times a week, is facilitated by an individual who has the responsibility to keep the meeting focused on getting suggestions proposed by fellow clients to help an individual learn what to change and how to change. Only the clients in the circle must offer suggestions on what and how to change. Staff and peer mentors are not permitted to offer suggestions. If a staff member or a peer mentor were to offer a suggestion, the clients would stop participating and let the staff or peer mentors run the meeting. It would no longer be peer-driven.

The whole structure of the model is to **role model appropriate social skills for positive change**. One alcoholic/addict who has made positive changes demonstrates through his or her action appropriate behavior for others to follow. This is the power of the model. Clients see the behavior change that they want to be demonstrated by one of their peers. This is a powerful motivational tool for change.

The entire campus of The Healing Place is one large community with multiple levels of activity. The process of change requires **accountability twenty-four hours a day, seven days a week.** For this accountability to occur, it requires everyone to understand that "if nothing changes, then nothing changes." Everyone realizes that, if they don't change, they will end up in jail, the hospital, or dead. Change happens when they hold themselves and each other accountable for their behavior. This is not snitching but instead helping each other learn how to change.

Keeping the focus on recovery is a daily task for the clients and the staff. There are many activities and services that could be added to the social model of recovery. Anything added to the model must be questioned as to its relevance to the model. Anything that has the potential to detract from the focus on recovery would ultimately, over time, make the model ineffective. Stay focused on only those tasks that support recovery.

It is crucial to continually address the fact that this is a **life and death issue**, and, if change does not occur, the ultimate end is death.

The overnight shelter and the detox unit are programs of entitlement. Everyone is entitled to a safe place to sleep and a safe place to withdraw from the effects of alcohol and or drugs. The recovery part of the model is about *empowering* the client to achieve sobriety, and the whole program is strength-based, allowing the individual to exercise **self-determination.** Focusing on the strength of each individual builds self-respect and self-confidence. To eliminate or reduce barriers facing the clients, all of the services provided by the social model recovery program at no cost to the client.

This model is a **program of attraction where peers relate to peers** through the change process. The peer mentor who is teaching a class at the off-site classroom becomes a beacon of hope for those wanting to change. That peer mentor is role-modeling positive behavior, and those observing are attracted to that individual because they want what that person has. It's all about attraction.

Because of the size of the program (one hundred beds or larger), it's impossible for the staff to govern the behavior of the community. Therefore, the responsibility for maintaining a safe and positive culture rests with the clients themselves. **Self-governance** is the key to a healthy environment.

Peer teaching is the most credible form of sharing what and how to change. A client/peer who has made behavioral changes can share with authority how they were able to make those changes with authority. This is extremely powerful because the source is believable. Individuals who are role-modeling positive recovery become an example for others to follow.

Because the clients themselves do all day-to-day living chores, it provides an opportunity to be responsible for a job and be willing to be held accountable for the performance of that job. This may be the first time they have an opportunity to **work on a team** and learn teamwork or leadership skills. It's okay to make a mistake on the job, but it is essential to take the opportunity to learn from that mistake. There is not a mistake happening at The Healing Place, where the consequences would be fatal. The same mistake on the street could get one killed. The Healing Place model is a safe place to make mistakes and learn from those mistakes.

Throughout the entire model, there are many opportunities for everyone to **share their experience, strength, and hope**. This is encouraged at all levels of the model. This is the power of peer-to-peer support and sharing unconditional love for one another.

During the community meeting, held in the middle of the week, client-supervisors are elected by the community. Using Robert's Rule of Order, the nominating and electing process is used to **elect clients to supervisory positions**, monitoring different work areas such as laundry, housekeeping, kitchen, clothing closet, landscaping, fire watch, housemaster, maintenance, and painting. Experience is not required to become a client supervisor; in fact, it's often a great learning opportunity for a client who is a people-pleaser or someone who has trouble delegating tasks.

Sprinkled throughout the model are opportunities for **physical and mental rewards for positive action and demonstrated motivation**. These rewards could be in the form of a bed move or a weekend pass. It's not enough to know that you are changing behavior; it's important to receive tangible rewards for that change.

Incumbent in the social model is the **responsibility for yourself and others**. You have the responsibility for your own change process as well as helping others change. Recovery is a "we" program rather than an "I" program.

The social model program focuses on **self-paced individualized progress** through the *Sober 180* curriculum. All clients go through the same process of attending classes and meetings but at their own pace. This is a treatment protocol. This treatment protocol differs from an individualized treatment plan found in the traditional clinical model of drug and alcohol treatment.

Again, the model is based on the **goal of recovery and is focused** on the steps necessary to accomplish that goal.

To help maintain a safe environment, there are five cardinal rules of **zero tolerance**. They are: no use of drugs or alcohol on campus, no violence or threats of violence, no racism, no sexually acting out, and no stealing. Any violation of any one of these rules is cause for immediate discharge from the program and to become ineligible for services and be ushered off the campus. During the following week, the appropriate staff will write a behavioral contract for the individual who violated the rule. If the violator can present proof of satisfactorily completing the behavioral contract, he or she will become eligible for services again. Swift execution of this policy sends a message to the street that The Healing Place takes immediate action when safety is jeopardized.

One of the key principles of the social model recovery program is **meeting the people where they are** and raising the bar of expectations. Do not judge the book by its cover. Do not assume "low expectations because of ignorance or biases." Everyone has strengths and abilities. If you expect more, you get more. The model recognizes that everyone has baggage and life issues. The challenge is to help the alcoholic/addict learn how to live sober and, through that process, gain strength and courage to face all these issues without relapsing.

Throughout the community, people often say, "I love him/her to death." In this social model, the strength-based statement would be, **"I love him/her to life."** The focus of the social model recovery program is to restore people to meaningful and productive lives. In other words, the mission is to love them to life.

Because this is a peer-driven community at all levels of service, the emphasis is on **"I am my brother's/sister's keeper."** We recognize that we are responsible to and for each other in helping all of us to learn how to live sober lives. I will get what I give, and the blessing is in the giving.

Love and support on the street last only if the drugs and alcohol are present. Once they are gone, there is no love or support. Alcoholics and addicts have learned over time that usually love costs and hurts. **Unconditional love** for the individual is difficult to understand. In the social model, this unconditional love without expectation is freely given, because it is recognized that if I don't love and help this individual, they may not live. "I may not like you today, but because I love you, I will look past our differences and reach out to help you change, and not expect anything in return for that love." This unconditional love allows the clients to confront inappropriate behavior in a loving and non-threatening way; it is supporting the individual for positive change to save their lives.

The long-term, intense, residential social model recovery program in a sheltered community is successful because it takes an average of six to nine months to complete all the requirements. The model is successful because the teacher and trainers are alcoholics and addicts who have made behavioral changes that they are willing to share with others. The model is credible because alcoholics and addicts are helping each other. Most of the clients in this type of model have had multiple treatment failures in some of the best treatment programs in the country. The message they come away with is that "I've been at the best, but I still relapsed. I'm hopeless to change, and I can't change." Peer alcoholics and addicts are making changes because of the peer-to-peer relationship of unconditional love without expectation and confronting behavior.

Prevention education is an essential part of the model in that successful alumni can share their experience, strength, and hope with school-age young people. The demand for drugs and alcohol is being reduced by the number of men and women achieving sobriety. These men and women are becoming role models for their families and children. Through the role-modeling of a meaningful and productive life, recovery is making a positive impact on the community at large.

The social model of recovery is based on the principle of service on demand, providing unlimited access to services offered by the model. There are limitations to the types of services provided in the social model of recovery. Clients presenting with serious and complicated medical issues and seriously decompensating mental health issues would be inappropriate for the peer-driven, mutual-help social model of recovery. When it is appropriate, referrals will be made to mental health programs and medically assisted treatment programs.

My Vision for the Future of The Healing Place

The Healing Place will continue to **reach** individuals suffering from drug and alcohol addiction, provide the tools for **recovery**, and **restore** meaningful and productive lives. The Healing Place will advocate for abstinence-based, peer-driven social model recovery. The Healing Place will provide a complete continuum of care, from detox to permanent supportive housing. The Healing Place's abstinence-based, long-term, residential, peer-driven social model of recovery will be replicated in 200 cities across the United States and abroad.

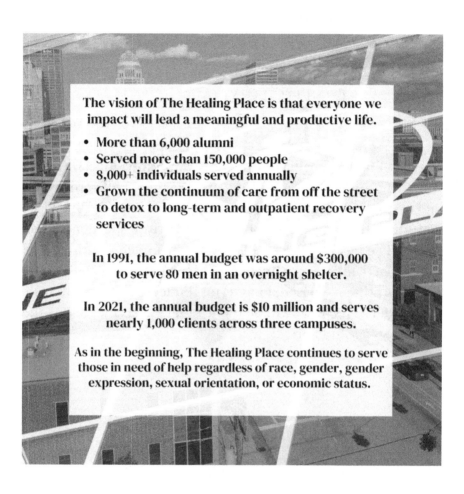

The vision of The Healing Place is that everyone we impact will lead a meaningful and productive life.

- More than 6,000 alumni
- Served more than 150,000 people
- 8,000+ individuals served annually
- Grown the continuum of care from off the street to detox to long-term and outpatient recovery services

In 1991, the annual budget was around $300,000 to serve 80 men in an overnight shelter.

In 2021, the annual budget is $10 million and serves nearly 1,000 clients across three campuses.

As in the beginning, The Healing Place continues to serve those in need of help regardless of race, gender, gender expression, sexual orientation, or economic status.

Review Inquiry

Hey, it's Jay here.

I hope you've enjoyed the book, finding it both useful and meaningful. I have a favor to ask you.

Would you consider giving it a rating wherever you bought the book? Online book stores are more likely to promote a work when they feel good about its content, and reader reviews are a great barometer for a book's quality.

So, please go to the website of wherever you bought the book, search for my name and the book title, and leave a review. If able, perhaps consider adding a picture of you holding the book. That increases the likelihood your review will be accepted!

Many thanks in advance,

Jay P. Davidson

WILL YOU SHARE THE LOVE?

Get this book for a friend, associate, or family member!

If you have found this book valuable and know others who would find it useful, consider buying them a copy as a gift. Special bulk discounts are available if you would like your whole team or organization to benefit from reading this. For more information, just visit TheHealingPlace.org/miracle.

WOULD YOU LIKE JAY P. DAVIDSON TO SPEAK TO YOUR ORGANIZATION?

Book Jay Now!

Jay P. Davidson accepts a limited number of speaking engagements each year. To learn how you can bring his message to your organization, please email Events@TheHealingPlace.org.

ABOUT THE AUTHOR

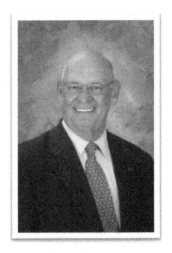

JAY P. DAVIDSON
MSSW, ACSW, LCSW, LCADC, MAC

After twenty years in the US Army, Jay retired as a lieutenant colonel, having had a successful career in the Infantry and Logistics. Post-retirement, Jay became a licensed real estate agent and worked two years as a property manager. He then served two years in Saudi Arabia as a civilian logistics consultant to the Royal Saudi Air Defense Force from 1988 to 1990. During his military career, Jay received the Legion of Merit, the Meritorious Service Medal, a Silver Star, a Bronze Star for

Valor, a Bronze Star for Meritorious Service, and four Army Commendation Medals.

In the spring of 1990, Jay entered the University of Louisville at the Kent School of Social Work and earned a master's degree in Social Work. He has extensive experience in chemical dependency and related mental health issues, family advocacy programs, and domestic violence.

Jay served as executive director / chief clinical officer of The Healing Place from 1991 to 2004. During that time, he developed the organization from an emergency overnight shelter into a full continuum of social and medical outreach initiatives for homeless men and women. Those who choose to enter the program are given an opportunity to break the cycle of homelessness, find recovery from chemical dependency, and return to their families and to the community as contributing members.

Jay served as president and chief executive officer of The Healing Place from 2004 to 2012. He has served as executive chairman since 2013 and continues to share the message of the nationally recognized and award-winning model addiction recovery program.

Jay lives in Louisville with his wife, Jackie, and has seven children, twelve grandchildren, and five greatgrandchildren.

Jay can be reached at: TheHealingPlace.org/contact-us.

Made in the USA
Las Vegas, NV
21 July 2021

26822556R00095